DR BHIMRAO AMBEDKAR
A COMPLETE BIOGRAPHY

AF552873

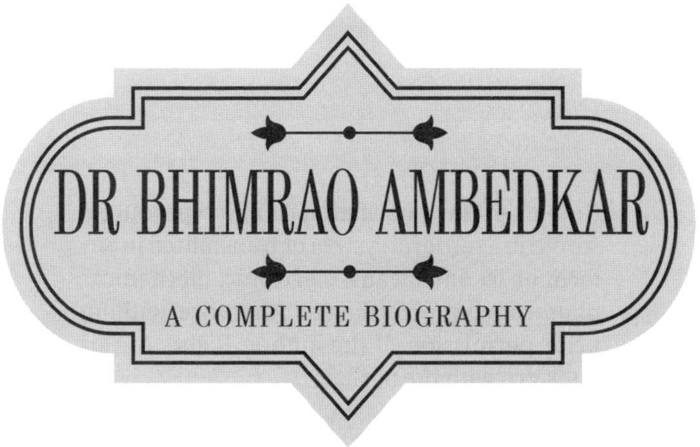

DR BHIMRAO AMBEDKAR

A COMPLETE BIOGRAPHY

PANKAJ KISHORE

PRABHAT
PRAKASHAN

No part of this publication can be reproduced, stored in a retrieval system or transmitted in any form or by any means, electronic, mechanical, photocopying, recording or otherwise, without prior permission of the author. Rights of this book are with the author.

Published by
PRABHAT PRAKASHAN PVT. LTD.
4/19 Asaf Ali Road,
New Delhi-110002 (INDIA)
e-mail: prabhatbooks@gmail.com

ISBN 978-93-5521-122-4
DR BHIMRAO AMBEDKAR A COMPLETE BIOGRAPHY
by Pankaj Kishore

© Reserved

Edition
2024

Price
₹ 300 (Rupees Three Hundred Only)

Printed at
Errorless Books Pvt. Ltd., Noida

Dedicated to the
Power of Constitution of India

Contents

Childhood and Education

Bhimrao Ramji Ambedkar was born on April 14, 1891 in Mhow Cantonment, Indore (MP). He was the 14th child of his parents. Of the 14 children, only 4 daughters and 2 sons survived. Bhimrao Ambedkar's father's name was Ramji Maloji Sakpal and mother's name was Bhimabai. Bhimrao's family hailed from Ambedkar village in Mandangarh of Ratnagiri district. He belonged to the Mahar caste—a caste in Maharashtra whose history is replete with tales of valour and courage. Some people of this caste used to remove dead animals from the villages.

Dr Ambedkar's grandfather Maloji Sakpal had retired from the Indian Army as a constable. His father Ramji was the headmaster of an army school which was run for the children of military personnel for 14 years. When Ramji worked in Mhow Cantonment in Madhya Pradesh, his most talented son Bhimrao was born. Everyone affectionately called him 'Bhima'.

Bhimrao's (Bhima) father Ramji Subedar retired from the army in 1893 after serving for 25 years. He lived with his family in Dapoli near his native village Ambadawe. As a young child, Bhima used to play many games with the children of his village. He loved to climb trees; at times, he even fought with the other children. Every day, people arrived with some complaint about Bhima; but Bhima unaware of these things, enjoyed his childhood. He didn't know what future had in store for him.

Bhima's life was full of obstacles. The first such obstacle occurred in 1894. The Municipal Education Department of Dapoli decided that it would not admit the untouchable children to its school. Ramji and other retired soldiers raised their voice against this injustice, but they did not succeed. Eventually, Ramji had to move to Bombay with his family. Life in Bombay was not easy for a person like Ramji, especially when he was an unemployed and retired untouchable person. Being a soldier, he somehow got a job in the PWD Satara office as a 'storekeeper'.

Bhimrao's formal education began on November 7, 1900. He got admission in the Satara Higher Secondary School after many difficulties. In those days, no one wanted to give admissions to untouchable children. In this school too, Bhima was given admission on the condition that he would not sit on the bench with other children in the class and that he would bring a mat and sit on it near the door. This condition was very offensive, but Bhima's father explained to him that education was the only solution to all their miseries and that he should concentrate only on his studies without paying attention to such hindrances or obstacles. But Bhima had to face difficulties every day. Often, he would cry because those difficulties were not easy to bear. After all, he was just a small child. Once a sensitive teacher asked him to solve a 'theory' on the blackboard. But many children opposed it. When the teacher could not understand the reason for this objection, those children explained the reason for their protest saying that how could a 'Mahar' write on the blackboard, which was near the place where their lunch boxes were kept. Bhima was allowed to write on the blackboard only after the children had removed their lunch boxes from there. This incident made a deep impact on young Bhima's mind.

The Principal of Satara High School was a gentleman. Though he was a Brahmin, he admitted the untouchable boy to his school regardless of caste distinction. He always encouraged Bhima. When Bhima could not go home to eat, he would personally bring food specially for him and persuade him to eat. It was he who gave him the last name 'Ambedkar', which came after the name Bhimrao. It was a rare act of kindness for the mistreated child, which he did not forget for the rest of his life.

Bhima had to face many problems in Satara. No barber would cut his hair because he was an untouchable. Once Dr Ambedkar's father, Subedar Ramji, was sent to help in the drought-prone area of Goregaon region. Schools were closed due to the drought. Bhimrao accompanied his brother Anandrao to the camp where his father worked. They reached Goregaon by train. But the area where his father worked was far from the station. They asked for a ride from the bullock carts that were going there. But none of the bullock cart drivers were prepared to give the untouchable children a ride in their cart. Finally, a carriage man agreed to give them a ride on the condition that they would drive the cart and that he would sit at the back and relax. Bhima had to drive the bullock cart for a day and a half, that too while remaining thirsty because the untouchables could not drink water from the village wells. Both the brothers reached the father's camp, completely exhausted.

Subedar Ramji began living with his family in Bombay in a rented room in a chawl in Lower Parel. By now, Bhima had passed out of the fourth standard. Bhima was enrolled in a government school called Elphinstone High School in Bombay. When Bhima was six years old, his mother died. Bhima's father had difficulties balancing his job and raising the children. He remarried a widow named Jijabai. When he started to live in Bombay, Bhima could not accept the presence of this 'new person' between himself and his father. He wanted his father's full love and attention. He would get very angry when he saw his stepmother wearing his mother's jewellery. Disturbed by the daily quarrels, one day, Bhima ran away from home. But he soon returned because he learnt that the outside world was worse than the environment at home. Now he paid full attention to his studies. He went to the garden at Charni Road and read books. His teacher, Shri Krishnaji Keluskar, also visited Bhima's that garden. He was very impressed by young Bhima's dedication. He would interact with Bhima and gave him many valuable suggestions.

Dr Ambedkar passed the matriculation examination in 1908. He was the first child from the Mahar community to pass that examination. The people of Mahar caste, who lived near his chawl, congratulated him on his achievement. Renowned social reformer and Marathi writer Shri A.K. Keluskar gifted Bhima a book on Gautam Buddha in Marathi, Mahatma Gautam Buddha Charitra, which he had written. He also got him a monthly stipend of ₹ 20. This stipend was given to him by the Maharaja of Baroda and educationist Shri Sayajirao Gaikwad for his further education.

Bhimrao Ambedkar was married to Ramabai. Ramabai was the daughter of Bhikhu Vanandkar. At that time, he was 17 years old and his wife was only 10 years old. After marriage, he began to be called 'Bhima'.

Most of the students studying at Elphinstone College were affluent. Bhima was very popular among his professors. He had a good knowledge of English and Persian languages. The English professor Mueller was so close to Bhima that he even gave him his shirt to wear. Bhima obtained his degree in 1912. He scored 282 marks out of 750 but could not secure first rank. Yet it was a great achievement for a man who had grown up in the midst of poverty and discrimination on account of caste. Everybody was very happy. Bhima never forgot his father's support and sacrifices that he had made for his education.

❑

First Job and Departure for America

During the time when Dr Ambedkar passed his graduation, his father's health was deteriorating. He had fever. He realised that the time had come to repay the debt for his father's sacrifices. He decided that he would take up a job and went to the for Maharaja's office in Bombay. It was the same Maharaja who had given him the stipend. Dr Ambedkar took the job of lieutenant in the army of Baroda. Just a few days after he had joined, he received a telegram informing him about his father's illness. He realised that his father had only a few days left but he did not get leave of absence. After all, it had been only 15 days since he had joined. He resigned from his job and went to meet his father for the last time. It seemed as if his father was also waiting for his Bhima. Ramji died on February 2, 1913.

The death of his father was a great shock to Dr Ambedkar. The responsibility of his large family had also fallen on his shoulders. He did not have a job at that time. It was then that he came to know that the Maharaja of Baroda paid for further studies of bright students at Columbia University (USA). His guru Shri Keluskar encouraged him to apply for the stipend. Dr Ambedkar was unwilling to seek further help from the Maharaja, but he had no other option. In order to be able to opt for higher studies, he had to promise in writing that after completing his studies, he would work in the state of Baroda for ten years.

On June 21, 1913, Dr Ambedkar arrived in the USA. He enrolled at Columbia University, where he lived at the Hartley Hall Residency. He later moved to the Cosmopolitan Club at 564 West, 114 Street where some Indian students also stayed. He eventually moved to the Livingstone Hall Residency, where he met Naval Bhathena, a Parsi , who was his room-mate and remained his lifelong friend.

Living in the USA proved to be a great respite for Dr Ambedkar. In the USA, no one asked questions about his untouchable caste. He had every sort of freedom. He could watch movies, eat and drink; in short, he could do whatever he wanted. But he had neither money nor desire to chase these worthless pursuits. He only concentrated on his studies. He sent a part of his stipend to his wife in India, who had to take care of his large family alone.

Dr Ambedkar ate only when he felt hungry. Still, he developed a strong and healthy body as he exercised regularly. The American people were quite impressed by his attractive physique.

America's friendly environment led to the development of many other qualities in him. He gained linguistic skills and developed his outlook. He once said, "We must reject the fatalistic view that the parents who give birth to children are not the only ones responsible for the actions of their children, but we must inculcate the concept that the parents alone are responsible for the future of their children. If girls are also educated along with their brothers, we will progress soon."

Senior professors such as John Dewey, James Howe Shotwell, Edwin Seligman, James Harvey Robinson, Franklin Giddings and Alexander Golden Wager had a profound impact on Ambedkar. He was very close to and influenced by John Dewey. Babasaheb Ambedkar studied subjects such as history, sociology, anthropology, philosophy, psychology and economics. The subject-matter of his study was always Indian subjects. During the MA, he wrote his research paper on 'Administration and Finance of the East India Company' and during the PhD, the topic of his research was 'The Evolution of Provincial

Finance in British India'. He completed his MA in 1915 and obtained his PhD from Columbia University in 1916.

For Baba Saheb, untouchability and apartheid (i.e., difference between white and black people) were two separate issues.

India's independence movement was in full swing at that time. When Lala Lajpat Rai visited America to garner support for the independence movement, he also urged Baba Saheb to participate in the freedom struggle. But Babasaheb rejected his offer because he wanted to complete his studies first. According to Baba Saheb, 'The Harijans of India are fighting for their fundamental rights. For them, this fight of caste difference is no less important than the fight for India's independence'. Lala Lajpat Rai understood his compulsion and did not press him further. Babasaheb spent three important years in America. The knowledge that he acquired during his stay there made a major contribution to the formation of his personality later on.

❑

Return to India

Dr Bhimrao Ambedkar wanted to study law and political science. So, he decided to move to London, where he enrolled at Gray's Inn to study law and economics and Political Science University in London to study economics. Meanwhile, he wrote a letter to the treasurer of Baroda asking that his monthly stipend be sent to his London address. But the officers there were not prepared to extend his stipend. He was asked to return to India immediately.

Dr Ambedkar felt dejected by these new circumstances and grudgingly had his luggage sent to Bombay through Thomas Cook and Sons; he left for home by the ship Kesar-e-Hind. It is said that difficulties never come alone. The ship which carried his luggage sank in the middle of the sea. Among his belongings were many of his valuable books, which he had collected during his stay in America. Dr Ambedkar returned to Bombay, India on August 21, 1917.

According to the contract, Dr Ambedkar was to go to Baroda, but he did not have the money to go there. Then he received the good news that he had received an insurance of ₹ 2000 due to the loss of his belongings. He gave some money to his wife and left for Baroda. He had sent the information of his arrival via telegram to Baroda. Maharaja Sayajirao Gaekwad of Baroda was very happy with the news. He asked his officers to receive Dr Ambedkar and his brother at the station. But no one went to receive them. After all, why would anyone receive the untouchables? Both the brothers kept looking for a place to stay in the city. Eventually they decided not to reveal their caste. Thus, they found a Parsi hotel to stay in.

Dr Ambedkar got the job of secretary in the Maharaja's army. It was an honourable appointment. But the Maharaja's peons and clerks did not think so. They would throw his files on the table so that they would not be touched by an untouchable person. Dr Ambedkar was never given water in the office. He used to spend his free time in the library.

Despite this partisan treatment, he never lost his calm and patience. Meanwhile, the owner of the hotel where he stayed came to know about his caste and threw him out of the hotel. Dr Ambedkar informed the Maharaja about his housing problem. The Maharaja spoke to his diwan about it. But the diwan expressed his helplessness saying that he could not help Ambedkar. Dr Ambedkar was deeply saddened by his circumstances. He felt that even higher education could not help him get rid of the discrimination that he faced owing to his caste and that even today people considered him as an untouchable.

In 1917, he decided to return to Bombay. While he was in Bombay, he told his mentor and adviser Shri Keluskar about this partisan treatment being meted out to him. Professor Joshiji, a friend of Shri Keluskarji, was in Baroda. He agreed to host Dr Ambedkar in his house. But when Dr Ambedkar reached Baroda, he received a letter sent by Joshiji at the station stating that his wife did not want to have an untouchable person in the house. Dr Ambedkar immediately took a return ticket to Bombay. He didn't want to face any more humiliation.

In Bombay, he was asked to participate in the conferences for the untouchables. However, he refused as it was necessary for him to find a job at the time. He had to accept many small jobs and also worked as a stock adviser. But when people came to know about his caste, they stopped going to him. In the meantime, Dr Ambedkar wrote a critical article for the famous British philosopher Bertrand Russell's book Principles of Social Reconstruction, which was published in the 'Indian Economics Society'. Similarly, many of his articles and essays appeared in reputed journals. However, he was still waiting for a respectable job.

Eventually, luck smiled upon him. He learnt about a vacancy for the post of lecturer at Sydenham College of Commerce and Economics, Bombay. He immediately applied for the position. He also cited Prof. Edwin Conan's reference. There were many eligible candidates for the post, but Dr Ambedkar was selected. Despite belonging to an untouchable caste, he was appointed as a temporary professor of economics because of his special abilities. He joined on November 11, 1918 at the monthly salary of ₹ 450. Initially, the students did not show any interest in attending the class of a lecturer from an untouchable caste. But Ambedkar continued to do his work with absolute devotion and dedication and soon became known for his extensive knowledge.

His closeness and familiarity with the students increased. The students were eager to attend his lectures. Even students from other colleges attended his lectures. His colleagues who used to discriminate against him gradually gave up that partisan behaviour. He was now familiar with the path of the struggle for equality.

In his spare time, he visited the nearby backward areas and spread awareness among the backward and downtrodden people, sensitising them about their rights.

During that time, he was introduced to Chhatrapati Shahuji Maharaj of Kolhapur in Maharashtra, who was a descendant of Chhatrapati Shivaji and sympathised with the people of the backward castes. He appreciated their significant contribution to Shivaji's army. He would constantly encourage Dr Ambedkar to work for the people of the Dalit caste and for their advancement. He asked Dr Ambedkar to bring out a magazine, which would help in this work. He brought out a Marathi fortnightly paper called Mooknayak on January 31, 1920. He personally collected donations for this magazine.

Dr Ambedkar still rued the lack of the degree which he could not obtain from London. He inquired at the University of London whether he could still get admission. His happiness knew no bounds when he learnt that he could still go to London to study. Dr Ambedkar resigned from his professorship on July 5, 1920 and prepared to go to London. He borrowed ₹ 5,000 from his friend Naval Bhathena. He also took some financial help from Shahuji Maharaj of Kolhapur.

❑

Departure to London

Dr Ambedkar reached London in July 1920 to study law and economics, taking full advantage of this opportunity. Along with his studies, he also took admission to the library of the London Museum. The library had a large collection of books and periodicals, which was very useful to him. He spent a lot of time in the library. He also started visiting the Indian Office Library and the University of London Library.

Dr Ambedkar stayed as a paying guest in London. He ate only twice a day—once in the morning and once in the evening. He spent most of his time reading. Once someone advised him to rest. Dr Ambedkar said, "I have neither money, nor food, nor time to sleep."

Dr Ambedkar was always sensitive to the condition of the Dalits in India and their progress. He was in constant touch with his co-workers and mentored them from time to time.

Those days Dr Ambedkar was going through a financial crisis. Most of his money was spent on buying books. By then he had finished his PhD from the American University. He had also obtained MSc, DSc and a degree in law from the University of London. He thought that it was the right time for him to return to India.

❑

Fight for Equality

Dr Ambedkar had married Ramabai in 1908. But he had not spent time with his wife. He was busy with his studies, job and social-reformation activities. Ramabai quietly continued to take care of his family. He realised the sacrifices made by his wife. Even when he was abroad, he used to send money from his savings to his wife. Dr Ambedkar had two sons—Gangadhar and Yashwantrao. Gangadhar died of a disease in his childhood. Like every father, he would worry about the health and education of his only son Yashwantrao.

Dr Ambedkar started his career as an advocate in the Bombay High Court in July 1923. But there too, the lawyers were not prepared to cooperate with the counsel from the untouchable caste. He only got cases of people belonging to the backward castes and lower strata. He managed to eke out a living from such cases. Gradually, his financial condition improved. Now, he felt the need for an institution which would run a movement for the progress of the Dalit community.

Meanwhile, he was approached with a defamation case. The case was against three writers named Bagde, Jeche and Jawalkar. The three writers belonged to the lower stratum and had written a book entitled Enemies of Country, in which they had blamed the Brahmins for the plight of the country. According to them, Brahmins divided the society into different classes through untouchability, social exploitation, malpractices and casteism and that they had imposed their agenda on the Hindus. The Hindu

Reform Programme had also confirmed the same. After hearing Dr Ambedkar's arguments, the court rejected the 'petition' of the Brahmins of Pune and the case was dismissed. That case was a personal victory for Dr Ambedkar. The Dalit people of the country now saw him as their leader—a leader who would free them from the life of untouchability. Dr Ambedkar founded the Bahishkrit Hitkarini Sabha for the development of Dalits on July 20, 1924. The first president of this organisation was a Gujarati Hindu and famous lawyer Sir Chimanlal Hiralal Setalvad. Dr Ambedkar was the chairman of the executive committee and also included some upper caste Hindus in the executive committee of the society.

The society organised conferences in every province of Maharashtra. The third conference of the society was held on April 10 – 11, 1925. Delivering a speech at the conference held in Nipani district in Belgaum, Dr Ambedkar said, "Mahatma Gandhi does not lay as much emphasis on the upliftment of Harijans as on Hindu–Muslim unity and on the use of khadi."

He urged people to fight for their rights. Citing the examples of America and France, he said, "Thousands died, but the next generation enjoyed the benefits. If we make sacrifices now, our future generations will be able to enjoy its benefits. In our community, the parents get their children married, but they do not ensure if their children are independent or not. That is why they become the cause of the poor circumstances of their children."

The society also had an impact on the Dalit movement and the society became the platform for the Dalit movement. The organisation started many hostels for the Dalits and brought out a magazine called Saraswati Vilas. In 1927, Babasaheb was appointed a member of the Bombay Legislature. Babasaheb brought great honour to this new position. In his welcome address, he also criticised the budget of that time in the assembly. Once he even gave evidence to the Home Minister Houston, that the police commissioner had refused to appoint untouchables in the police force although there was no such provision in the law. The Dalit movement progressed under the leadership of a capable leader like Dr Ambedkar.

Babasaheb Ambedkar kept this Dalit movement secluded from religious, political and social movements. It was during that time that Babasaheb came to know about a bill, according to which it was legal for the untouchables to take and use water from common sources. Harijans could draw water from places like wells, ponds and rivers. The untouchables had a legal right to draw water from these common sources.

With the help of this new law, Babasaheb fought for the right of the untouchables to drink water from common sources. He started this fight from Mahad because he knew that area.

The Mahad Conference was organised on March 19, 1927, in which five thousand people participated to free the Chavdar Lake. People from Gujarat and Maharashtra gathered at Mahad. On that day, Babasaheb Dr Ambedkar offered three new resolutions—not to eat the flesh of dead beings, not to consume the leftovers from people's plates, and behave like middle class people without worrying about his caste barriers and adopt their lifestyle.

At the same conference, it was also decided that the water of Mahad Lake would be available to everyone irrespective of their castes as stated in the Municipal Judgement. Babasaheb reached Mahad Lake in a procession which went through the streets of Mahad. After reaching the lake, he drank a little water from it. After him, others drank water from the lake and returned to the conference room.

Some upper caste Hindus watched this incident. They tried to oppose it. After all, how could they let these untouchables touch the drinking water? They attacked the conference room when people were having a meal. Some people were also badly injured. Babasaheb was very angry. But he remained calm and suppressed his anger because he knew that it was time to be patient and take decisions. He asked the people present there not to protest and to continue with their work following the path of non-violence.

Dr Babasaheb Ambedkar's foresight saved the situation; otherwise, it would have become explosive because at this conference, many soldiers were also present who were from the army that had participated in the war of Afghanistan and other battles. They could have created dread for the opponents. When the police arrived, Babasaheb took the injured to the hospital. Five attackers were punished.

The Mahad Satyagraha proved to be a milestone for the Dalit movement. It was Dr Ambedkar's first major achievement. For the first time in history, the Dalits had undertaken a direct fight for their rights. The news of the conference spread like wildfire. People implemented the three resolutions taken at the conference. This also had a negative effect on the Dalits. They were socially boycotted in many villages. There was also a reaction to the incident across the country. But many social reformers like Veer Savarkar gave their full support to Dr Ambedkar.

❑

Many Struggles

In those days, Dr Ambedkar was not in favour of the mild stance of the press. He wanted to bring out a newspaper in order to raise the voice of the Dalits. On April 3, 1927, he started a fortnightly newspaper called Bahishkrit Bharat (The Excluded India). This newspaper, which lasted for a period of three years, raised its voice loudly for the Dalits.

Dr Ambedkar came to know that some Brahmins were purifying the water of Mahad

Lake. He was very angry. The second setback arose when a new decision was taken setting aside the previous decision, which said that the water of the Mahad lake would not be available for every caste for drinking purposes. Babasaheb decided to hold a satyagraha in protest against the decision. He asked all the workers of the society to participate in the satyagraha for the water of the Mahad Lake. Meanwhile, some upper caste Hindus brought an order from the civil court that Ambedkar and others should be stopped from holding the satyagraha. The court issued a notice in that regard.

Dr Ambedkar and the rest of the activists reached the Mahad Lake on foot without paying attention to the notice. The police were guarding the lake. When Dr Ambedkar reached there, the district magistrate sent a summon and asked to put an end to the conflict. Dr Ambedkar did not respond and returned to the venue of the conference where he was received by about fifteen thousand activists from several villages. He compared that convention to the national rally which was held in France on May 5, 1789. Dr Ambedkar said, "We also want to take action like them. The path which we have chosen is correct for the progress of Hindu society. The Hindu society will again have to walk on the path of the two principles—equality and the end of caste discrimination."

He asked the satyagrahis not to touch the Mahad tank because their fight was with the upper caste Brahmins and not with the government. He affirmed that their aim was to bring equality in the Hindu community. He also told the women present there that they should pay attention to their personal hygiene and attire. He observed that they should dress like upper class women and educate their children. All the women took Babasaheb's advice seriously and the next day, they came dressed neatly.

❑

Simon Commission and Round Table Conference

The Simon Commission headed by Sir John Simon arrived in India on August 3, 1928. The Congress Party boycotted it as it did not represent any Indian and it was not for the welfare of a common Indian. The people protested against the Simon Commission with black flags. People raised the slogan of 'Go back Simon'. During the protest, Lala Lajpat Rai was lathi-charged in Lahore. He was seriously injured and died on

November 17, 1928. On the death of Lala Lajpat Rai, Dr Ambedkar paid tribute by organising a condolence meeting.

Like some other Dalit organisations, Dr Ambedkar also thought that opposing the government would not be in the interest of the welfare of the Dalits. He met the commission and presented his demands on behalf of his society that worked for the interest of the downtrodden. He urged the commission to pay attention again to the education and development of the Dalits and also gave some suggestions which could improve their condition. As his second counteraction, he asked for 22 of the 140 seats in the legislature to be reserved for them. He also placed a 94-page 'memorandum' before the commission and then signed the Simon Report.

National leaders criticised Dr Ambedkar for his support to the Simon Commission. They felt that it was not in favour of the freedom movement. But when everyone saw the memorandum, they were very surprised to see Dr Ambedkar's national spirit. In that memorandum, all those issues which were in the interest of the country were taken care of. The national leaders were greatly impressed by Dr Ambedkar and he began to be recognised as a prominent leader of the country. Dr Ambedkar's influence began to increase. He started campaigning for the satyagraha that was to begin for the entry of untouchables into temples. That would have created a special place for the Dalits in Hindu society. In his first speech at the Dalit Conference held on December 28, 1929, he said, "Political might is needed to abolish untouchability. Political empowerment alone will improve our standard of living. Merely dressing like the upper class people is not progress. Real progress can only come from political power. According to the British Government, law cannot eradicate social discrimination. So, we should fight for national independence. I have no faith in the British Government. We have to become benevolent. The British Government is only business minded." People from Mahad, Chambar, Thor, etc., participated in this conference.

Dr Ambedkar's speech at Mahad was the culmination of his previous stand. He was not totally against the government as per the previous views; but now he was completely opposed to the government. He now wanted complete independence of the country and participated in the freedom movement along with other national leaders of the country. The second conference of the Dalits was organised on August 8, 1930. At this conference, it was decided that the representatives of the Dalits would also participate in the First Round Table Conference.

On November 12, 1930, Dr Ambedkar participated in the First Round Table Conference as a representative of Dalits. It was presided over by the British Prime Minister Ramsay McDonald. Dr Ambedkar presented the wretched condition of Dalits before the British Government. He said that the British Government had done very little for the advancement of the downtrodden and the oppressed classes although they formed a significant part of India's population. Through his speech, Dr Ambedkar provided an international platform to the Dalit problem. He returned to India on November 27, 1931.

❑

Influence of Mahatma Gandhi

Dr Ambedkar was once again invited to London for the Second Round Table Conference along with Mahatma Gandhi. Muhammad Ali Jinnah and Sir Tej Bahadur Sapru were also to attend the conference with him. Mahatma Gandhi still contemplated whether to attend the conference or not. Before participating in it, he wanted to meet Dr Ambedkar. Dr Ambedkar met him on August 14, 1931.

During the meeting, Mahatma Gandhi told Ambedkar that for him, the problems of the downtrodden were more important than Hindu–Muslim unity. It was he (Ambedkar) who did not allow him to address those issues properly. He said that he had spent ₹ 20 lakhs to end the discrimination. Dr Ambedkar instantly said, "I really don't know about it." He further said, "All such efforts on part of the Congress are like giving us new clothes to wear for festivals." When Gandhiji appreciated Dr Ambedkar's contribution made during the First Round Table Conference, Ambedkar became emotional and said, "You are talking to me about my motherland. No Dalit, who has even slight self-respect and humane spirit, would call this land his homeland, where he has to live in conditions worse than that of cats and dogs and he is not treated with sympathy which even animals are sometimes shown. You are raising a voice about the atrocities on farmers in Bardoli, but you cannot hear the problems and cries of Dalits. There is no system even in your national press which will inform the country about our troubles." The first meeting between Dr Ambedkar and Gandhiji was not smooth and it created a sense of disappointment between the two national leaders that never went away.

Before meeting Gandhiji, while addressing the youth of backward castes, Dr Ambedkar had openly criticised Gandhi's policies. He said, "I promise that I will always work for the upliftment of the untouchables. Ahmedabad was the centre of business till now; but after Gandhiji's arrival, only politics is talked about. I think you know more about politics than myself. I think that those who wear khadi don't really know about the power of Gandhiji's politics.

"Do they know all this? Can you win by sitting for satyagraha? Are the strong British rulers surrendering to Gandhiji? But I ask all the khadi wearers, what have you done for your progress? He asks you to participate in satyagraha for freedom. But what did he do to eradicate untouchability? What did he do for your right to draw water from wells? Many of my companions also hate me, but I don't care. You say that we should also do something for this country. But can we call this country ours? They don't even consider you human. They don't want you to have your own land. They don't want to allow you to walk on streets. How can you call this country yours? I went to the Round Table Conference for the benefit of the backward castes. But Gandhiji was also sent by the Congress, which was not right. He talks about the need for Hindu–Muslim unity or Hindu–Sikh unity, but why doesn't he speak about us untouchables?"

Dr Ambedkar added, "During that Round Table Conference, I argued for the country. I fought for the whole country, which no other Hindu did. I also want the freedom of my country like every individual. But first I want freedom of my caste; give me that freedom. Eradicating caste discrimination is most important for me."

On August 29, 1931, Dr Ambedkar participated in the Second Round Table Conference. On this occasion, due to his knowledge of law, he was appointed to the 'Federal Structure Committee'. Mahatma Gandhi also participated in the conference along with other colleagues from the Congress like Pandit Madan Mohan Malaviya, Sarojini Naidu, etc.

Dr Ambedkar placed the demand for adult franchise before the committee. He clarified, "If only a few people get the right to vote, then the government that will be formed will be of the minority, which will acquire the confidence that it will be responsible for the interests of the majority. For me, there are only two issues to be debated in this conference—will there be a responsible government in India? And if there will be, what will it be responsible for? I wonder why all those who want a responsible government do not want to give voting rights to the adult Indians." Mahatma Gandhi and other Congress leaders also demanded adult franchise.

"The right to vote should not be taken away from any adult Indian on the basis of his poverty and illiteracy. An educated person is intelligent and understands his own interests; but it is unjust that you cannot choose your representative because you are poor. A free democratic government should depend on the fact that the individual learns from his own experience."

In London, further ideological differences arose between Gandhiji and Ambedkar. Gandhiji was not prepared to consider Dalits a minority community and Ambedkar did not agree with his views. He said, "From my meetings with Gandhiji so far, I have understood that Gandhiji is not ready to consider Dalits and Anglo-Christians as minority communities. And if we do not have a constitutional right in the future, then we do not want to participate in any dialogue."

The information about the activities at the Second Round Table Conference spread like wildfire in India. The Dalits called a meeting and resolved that Dr Ambedkar was their representative. Then they sent telegrams about the decision to London.

Till the end, Dr Ambedkar held on to his demand that Dalits should also get the right of independent franchise. On August 20, 1932, the British Prime Minister announced the communal decision called 'Communal Award'. Under that, the Dalits were given the right of a separate electorate. Many prominent Dalit leaders like Rao Saheb and M.C. Raja had abandoned the idea. Rao Saheb Raja was the only representative of Dalits in the Central Legislative Assembly. Earlier he had demanded a separate electorate for Dalits in Punjab.

Mahatma Gandhi was in Yerwada Jail at that time. He warned the British Government that he would not accept the demand for a separate electorate for the backward castes and that if his words were not heeded, he would go on a hunger strike. Finally, Mahatma Gandhi started his fast unto death on September 20, 1932 in Pune. The whole country was stunned by Mahatma Gandhi's attitude. Leaders like Pandit Madan Mohan Malaviya tried to mediate to find a way out. They organised a conference, where Dr Ambedkar was also invited to participate. Dr Ambedkar was not willing to compromise on the issue. Some Indians, who were not in favour of Dr Ambedkar, even called him a traitor.

During the conference, Dr Ambedkar said, "It

is very sad that Gandhiji is not in favour of the rights of the backward and oppressed classes. He could have suggested some other option. But I am not prepared to accept any alternative which is not in the interest of the oppressed class just because it is a matter of Gandhiji's life."

Both Dr Ambedkar and Gandhiji were adamant on their respective stands. Many discussions were organised to persuade them. Many senior leaders such as Dr Ambedkar himself, Pandit Madan Mohan Malaviya, Chunilal Mehta, Rajagopalachari, Jayakar, Sapru, Birla and Mahatma Gandhi's son Devdas played an important role in that. They wanted the two leaders to agree on one point. There were many meetings between Dr Ambedkar and Gandhiji. Eventually, both leaders agreed that voting would take place and some seats would be reserved for the Dalits. This agreement between Dr Ambedkar and Mahatma Gandhi is known as the 'Poona Pact'.

The British cabinet placed this announcement

in the parliament. Dr Ambedkar reserved 148 seats for the Dalits. Earlier, only 71 seats were reserved for them. But the Dalits lost the right to choose their own representative and elect a Hindu representative.

Regarding the announcement of the Poona Pact, Subhas Chandra Bose said, "Dr Ambedkar had demanded separate franchise in the Round Table Conference, but got reserved seats. It would have been better if Gandhiji had agreed with him. Ambedkar's opinion was much better."

❑

Dr Ambedkar Undergoes Transformation

After the Poona Pact, the Dalit movement gained more momentum. Some small but important rights were given to the Dalits, such as entry to temples, eating together with Hindus, etc. Dr Ambedkar kept his focus on political rights. He said at a meeting, "Entering the temples will not make you liberal. Only the political rights can make you better." He told the people, "Maintain unity." Dr Ambedkar went to London to attend the Third Round Table Conference on November 7, 1932. He was not pleased with the attitude of the Muslim leaders. On his return, he met Gandhiji in Yerwada Jail.

In 1933, Ranga Iyer tried to obstruct the entry programme of a temple. He got the resolution passed in the Madras Legislative Assembly against it. Dr Ambedkar said in his defence, "The power of Dalits should not be wasted on these petty issues. Dalits can bring about their development by fighting for their rights. They can progress by getting higher education, higher appointments and respectable ways of earning a living. It is now up to you whether you allow them to enter the temples or not. If you have faith in humanity, then the doors of temples should be opened in view of democratic rights." He told the people not to worry about such matters. According to him, a case had to be made. Rather than praying, people should work and make themselves self-reliant. He said that people should be the creators of their own destiny.

Many Hindus did not approve of Dr Ambedkar's liberal views. Dr Ambedkar once again left for London, where at the conference he said, "I was very disappointed with the inhuman treatment meted out by Hindus to us. That is why I spoke of a separate franchise. If Hindus try to reform the society and bring about uniformity, then we will cooperate with them."

In 1933, Dr Ambedkar fought Dr R.D. Karve's case. Karve was the editor of a magazine entitled Samaj Swasthya. The magazine created awareness about sex among the people. Some of the material in the December 1933 issue of that magazine was deemed obscene and an officer sued Karve who was the magazine's editor.

Dr Ambedkar had always been a supporter of progressive ideas. He strongly defended Dr Karve. Dr Ambedkar was exhausted because of hard work. He took a few days off from work and travelled to Bordi, Mahabaleshwar and Panhalgarh. There he underwent naturopathy. Upon his return, he resumed his law practice and began teaching at the college.

He built his new house in the Dadar area of Mumbai, which he named 'Rajgriha'. Rajagriha was the capital of King Bimbasara during the Buddhist period. Babasaheb's wife was not well during those days. He didn't even get an opportunity to take care of his wife. Ramabai died on May 27, 1935. The death of his wife was a great shock to him. His wife had single-handedly taken care of the entire family. She had never asked Babasaheb for anything. As long as she was alive, Babasaheb was free from family worries. Babasaheb was left alone by her untimely demise. He was in such a state of shock that for some time he shaved his head and wore the clothes of a monk.

Many people thought that Babasaheb would retire from politics as well. But soon he lived his life as usual. On June 2, 1935, he was appointed as the Principal of the Law College, Bombay. He was also asked to hold the post of district judge, but he turned down the offer. He felt that society could be served better by being free from the tensions of a job.

During those days, he had to go to Mahad in connection with the Mahad Satyagraha case. He had to stop on the way for some time as the river was flooded and was forced to spend the day without food and water as there were no Dalit houses nearby. The people from Hindu castes were not prepared to offer food and water to a Dalit man.

Dr Ambedkar was enraged that even after being highly educated and undergoing struggle, people considered him an untouchable. Some Dalits wanted to convert to another religion. He urged them not to take any decision in haste. He was discouraged by the constant hostility from the Hindus. He felt that the struggle for the satyagraha to enter the temples was futile. According to him, the upper caste Hindus would never give them the right to equality. Dr Ambedkar declared at the Mewla Conference on October 13, 1935, "Unfortunately I was born a Hindu; it was not in my control. But I pledge that I will not die a Hindu." He said that he was a Hindu by chance and not by choice. He said that he wanted to give up or renounce the religion that did not give him the right to live with dignity. For the first time, Dr Ambedkar wanted to get converted. He asked his Dalit brethren to do the same.

After this announcement, many religious leaders urged him to adopt their religion. The Muslim Nizam of Hyderabad even spoke about giving him up to ₹ 5 crores if he and the rest of the Dalits adopted his religion. Christians, Sikhs and Buddhists also urged him to do the same.

Many Congress leaders strongly criticised Dr Ambedkar's decision to convert. Mahatma Gandhi said, "Untouchability is now in its last phase. Even if it is present in some places, it is not enough to incense an educated youth like Dr Ambedkar. Yet religion is not like an old house or old clothes which can be taken off and thrown away."

Dr Ambedkar said, "We have not decided which religion we will adopt. But after much deliberation we have come to the conclusion that Hindus won't let us progress.

"Religious inequality itself is the fault of this religion. I agree with Gandhiji that every person needs religion. But I am not ready to continue to follow the religion of my forefathers which does not allow an individual or community to progress."

Many Hindus also opposed the conversion of Dalits. Several political and religious Hindu leaders also urged Dr Ambedkar to drop the idea of conversion. He said that he was prepared to remain a Hindu, but before that Hindus would have to eradicate casteism.

Dr Ambedkar did not want individual conversion. He wanted mass conversion. For that, he started meeting people and spreading awareness through his speeches. At one such meeting, he said, "Progress requires one to be ambitious and completely optimistic. The person who has hopes, desires and goals is truly alive. The greatest duty of a person in life is to preserve the inner values and destroy the old beliefs and customs. Always be optimistic. You should be hard-working and honest. If the individual is righteous, then the community and the nation will get strength and that will be their fate."

At a conference held in Pune in January 1936, Dr Ambedkar said, "I will not change my decision about Dalit conversion even if God comes to reason with me. I want to get you out of your abject condition. I have a personal interest in this as well. You have to be accountable for your own responsibilities. If you follow me, you will become a liberal."

Despite being busy with the issue of conversion, he worked for many other important issues, such as his suggestion to turn the study of law into a degree course like other technical subjects. He suggested the addition of disciplines like sociology, psychology, logic and debate in legal studies as all these skills are essential for a lawyer.

In 1937, Dr Ambedkar also wrote a book, Annihilation of Caste. It is an important publication, in which he has presented solemn thoughts on casteism. Mahatma Gandhi too praised this book.

❑

Proposed Elections for the Formation of Government of India in the Year 1935

In 1935, the decision to form an independent government came into force in India. According to that decision, the provision for independent government in the state was given and states were asked to form independent governments. In August 1936, Dr Ambedkar founded a new party, which was named 'Swatantra Labour Party'.

In the declaration of this party, emphasis was made on the development of new industries and keeping the old ones running so that the landless labourers could be saved from exploitation.

Elections were to be held on February 17, 1937. Dr Ambedkar worked very hard for his new party. He addressed meetings in Igatpuri, Sinnar, Nashik, Nagar, Jalgaon, Satara, Solapur and Pune. His perseverance bore fruit. He won a majority and his party won 13 out of 17 seats.

Congress also won the election, but it was not prepared to form the government. The government asked Sir Dhanjishah Cooper and Jamnadas Mehta to form the cabinet. Congress requested Dr Ambedkar to sign the 'no-confidence motion', but he refused.

The Cooper government resigned on July 16, 1937 and the Congress government was formed. The Congress representatives and Dr Ambedkar took the oath. On September 17, 1937, he got a bill for the farmers passed. He was the first member to do so.

Meanwhile, Dr Ambedkar continued to struggle for the upliftment of Dalits. He declared at a meeting in Solapur, "Progress will not take place until casteism is eradicated. Economic exploitation will not end unless the poor ask the rich for their rights. This movement of our self-confidence alone will protect our interests."

Dr Ambedkar supported that resolution in the assembly. That proposal was put forth by Jamnadas Mehta. In that resolution, the interference of the government during the judicial system was opposed. In support of the proposal, he said, "The criminal court in India does not hear the appeal of the offender unless it has violated the judicial principles. This creates indifference and doubt in the minds of the people about the judicial system. Pardoning a criminal weakens the law. Has the home minister taken the chief minister's opinion in this regard?"

In May 1938, Dr Ambedkar resigned as the Principal of the Law College. During his visit to Konkan, he again urged the Dalits not to remove the skin of dead animals or eat their meat. Baba Saheb knew that in spite of his efforts to spread awareness, some people still indulged in such abominable acts.

❑

Years of War

In 1939, the Second World War had started because of Germany's invasion of Poland. India was also involved in this war. According to the Congress, dictators like Adolf Hitler and Mussolini proved to be dangerous for the world. Therefore, it was the first duty of every democratic country to fight against such dictators. Dr Ambedkar also wanted the British Government to fight against Germany. But he was not very happy with the attitude of the

Congress. According to him, the Congress was acting as if it was the only representative of India. Dr Ambedkar also wanted the British Government to clarify its post-war policy.

In October 1939, Lord Linlithgow, the Viceroy of India, discussed his post-war policy with the Congress and Dr Ambedkar. After the discussion, he declared that after the end of the war, many reforms would be implemented in India and that the opinion of every section would be taken into account. The Congress was not satisfied with the Viceroy's statement. It asked the provisional Congress ministers to resign.

Dr Ambedkar opposed the decision of the Congress. "Patriotism is not the legacy of the Congress alone. Other parties also have their own independent opinion," he said. He was also not happy with the attitude of the Muslim League.

That was the time when the Muslim League was promoting the idea of creation of a separate Muslim country. Dr Ambedkar wrote a book on the issue, Thoughts on Pakistan. The book was published in 1940. According to Dr Ambedkar, it would be in everybody's interest if the Muslims were allowed to have their own country. The Muslims were more religious and were against social reform. Islam is a major religion of the world and its principles are perpetual. Dr Ambedkar believed that diligent Hindu soldiers were necessary for India's security, not secure borders.

He gave examples of Turkistan, Greece and many other countries. According to him, if India wanted a powerful central government, it was very necessary to have a separate Muslim country. Both Mahatma Gandhi and Jinnah considered this book to be an effective medium to understand the India–Pakistan issue. The second edition of the book was published in 1945. At that time, its title was changed to 'Pakistan and the Partition of India'. In this book, the issue of partition was seen from a religious point of view, which the government, Congress and Muslim League were not taking seriously.

Dr Ambedkar was always in favour of appointing Mahars in the army. Around 1941, he urged the governor to form a new squad of Mahars called the Mahar Regiment.

Meanwhile, the British Government appointed Sir Cripps to solve India's political problem. The Cripps Mission came to India in 1942 and discussed political issues with the Congress, Muslim League and Hindu Mahasabha. Dr Ambedkar and M.C. Raja also met the mission. The Cripps Mission decided that a committee would be formed after the war to draft the Constitution of India.

The Congress, Muslim League and Hindu Mahasabha rejected the decision.

On April 14, 1942, Dr Ambedkar turned 50 years old. His party workers and followers celebrated his birthday with great fervour. A bag was also presented to him. However, Dr Ambedkar was opposed to pomp and show. On that occasion, he said, "If a person is worshipped like God with absolute devotion and faith, then that community starts moving towards degradation. No one is born with divine qualities. It is up to you as to which way you want to go—growth or decline. It depends on how you live your life."

1942 was a historic year. Mahatma Gandhi started the 'Quit India' movement. All the people opposed the British Government. The British Government was shaken by the protests on such a large scale. That year was also a historic year for Dalits, especially for Dr Ambedkar. For the first time, a Dalit, i.e. Dr Ambedkar was made a minister. Lord Linlithgow gave him the position of adviser to the Viceroy.

Lord Linlithgow was so angry with the Quit India Movement that he issued an order to arrest all the leaders and send them to Andaman Jail. Dr Ambedkar strongly opposed the Viceroy's order. He warned that the order to arrest all the leaders and send them to Andaman Jail would hurt the honour and dignity of the British Government and that the government should not adopt such undemocratic methods.

Mahatma Gandhi was arrested and kept in the Aga Khan Palace in Poona. Gandhiji started a fast from February 10, 1943. Some leaders resigned from the Viceroy's Committee in support of Gandhiji. But Dr Ambedkar retained his post.

The world war ended in 1945. The Allies won the war. Germany, Italy and Japan suffered humiliating defeats. Elections were held in Britain and the Labour Party assumed power.

The Labour Party was in favour of giving independence to India. Prime Minister Attlee sent the Stanford Cripps Mission. A.V. Alexander and Lord Pethick were also its members. The mission wanted a proactive procedure under which India could be given independence.

Prime Minister Attlee also wanted a satisfactory solution to the Hindu–Muslim problem.

It was decided that India would be divided into two countries—India and Pakistan, wherein Muslims would live in greater numbers in Pakistan. Mahatma Gandhi opposed the partition, but Dr Ambedkar supported it because he thought in that way the enmity between Hindus and Muslims would end.

Elections were declared for the formation of an interim government. The Congress and Muslim League put their representatives in the fray for the election. Dr Ambedkar also proposed representatives from his 'Republican Party of India'. Their representatives were few as the election was a battle of strength between the Congress and the League, between the Hindus and the Muslims. The voters voted on the basis of religion. It was the time for the Congress and the League to show their hold over India and accordingly ask for a separate country for themselves.

Dr Ambedkar was also elected to the Central Assembly from the Bengal Assembly as the representative of the Dalits. He was not happy with the attitude of the Congress. He observed that because of his poor relations with Mahatma Gandhi, the Congressmen did not leave any opportunity to curtail his rights.

On June 4, 1946, a meeting of the 'Dalit Federation' was organised. N. Shivraj led it. In it, the right of a 'separate region' was demanded for the Harijans, otherwise they would not get representation in the assembly or in the council. The interim government rejected this motion of the assembly.

The interim government accepted equal representation of Hindus and Muslims, but the Dalits were not given special representation. Dr Ambedkar opposed it. The Congress was not happy with his disapproval. Some misguided Congress supporters set fire to Dr Ambedkar's printing press.

On April 29, 1948, Sardar Patel introduced a bill for the abolition of untouchability, which was also passed. Untouchability was declared illegal in India. It was a big victory for Dr Ambedkar. He had devoted his whole life to it, but the press did not acknowledge his contribution.

❑

Freedom and the New Constitution

India became independent on August 1947. But India was divided into two countries—India and Pakistan. Pandit Jawaharlal Nehru took the oath as the prime minister.

Pandit Jawaharlal Nehru had always respected Dr Ambedkar for his wisdom and courage. He believed that Dr Ambedkar had a deep and solid knowledge of the law of the land.

He appointed Dr Ambedkar as law minister in the cabinet. It came as a surprise to Dr Ambedkar who gladly accepted the position.

On August 29, 1947, a committee was constituted to prepare the draft of the Constitution of new India. Dr Rajendra Prasad was made the chairman of this committee. Nehru asked Dr Ambedkar to preside over this committee. Other members also supported him in this work. He happily accepted the challenge.

When Dr Ambedkar started working on the draft, he felt that some members of the committee were not enthusiastic about him being made a member of the committee. He ignored them and started this important work with full responsibility. Within six months, he presented the draft of the Constitution to Dr Rajendra Prasad who was the speaker of the assembly. The draft of the Constitution had 315 articles and 8 appendices.

When Dr Ambedkar worked on the draft Constitution, his health deteriorated rapidly. He was in constant need of medical attention. During that time, he came in contact with Dr Sharda Kabir of Mavalankar Hospital in Bombay. He felt connected with her and decided to get married. He married for the second time on April 15, 1948. Now, he had a doctor in his house, who took care of his health.

Everyone was impressed with this great work by Dr Ambedkar which he had accomplished by drafting the Constitution. T .T. Krishnamachari in his speech to the assembly, praised his devotion, saying, "Of the seven members who were chosen to frame the Constitution, one resigned, one died, one went to America, one was busy with other work, one or two lived away from Delhi, some had to leave this work due to ill health. Dr Ambedkar alone had to handle this task."

In his historic speech while presenting the Constitution, he said, "The constitution that I am presenting can be good or bad, it depends on how it is used by the people in the office. India won its independence. India had lost its freedom because we were not united; those who were in power betrayed her."

Dr Ambedkar had long dreamed of reforming Hinduism. He worked on a special bill, which was presented as the 'Hindu Code Bill'. All fanatical Hindus opposed it. Those who had praised Dr Ambedkar for drafting the Constitution also started opposing him. Even Dr Rajendra Prasad was not prepared to support him. But Pandit Jawaharlal Nehru and Sarojini Naidu wanted this bill to become a law. However, because of strong opposition, he also withdrew his support and the bill never became a reality.

❑

Conversion to Buddhism

Dr Ambedkar was completely shattered after his dream in the form of the bill was broken. He felt that Dalits would never get their rights as long as they followed Hinduism. He made up his mind that he would adopt Buddhism. He was interested in Buddhism because he thought that Islam and Christianity considered Indian culture to be different. He thought that Buddhism was a more modern and liberal religion. He once wrote in an article titled 'Rise and Fall of Hindu Women',

"The freedom that Hindu women enjoyed during the Buddhist period was 'unannihilated'." He further wrote, "Buddha considered women to be parivrajakas or bhikshunis; so, he gave them freedom to attain enlightenment. They also got the right to self-development. Buddha revolutionised the whole community. He gave freedom and self-respect to women. Manu did not want to allow women to convert to Buddhism. He wanted to bind them in many ways and enslave them."

Dr Ambedkar began to feel lonely. He had faith in Nehru, but Nehru had also betrayed him. He did not find it ethical to continue in the government. He sent his resignation letter to Prime Minister Pandit Nehru on September 27, 1951. He wanted to talk about his resignation in the House, but the speaker did not give him an opportunity. Expressing his protest, he rose from the House and left. He gave his statement to the newspaper reporters standing outside.

He had said in his statement, "When society leaves the past behind and moves towards the future, then the true test for it is conscience. When society is surrounded by casteism and inequality, then to constantly talk about changing the society by making economic laws without touching Hinduism is a mockery of the Constitution and is like building a sand castle."

That was not the end of his political career. The first general elections were held in 1952. Dr Ambedkar contested from the Socialist Party. He was defeated, but he did not give up. In March 1952, he was elected as a member of the Rajya Sabha.

In May 1953, Dr Ambedkar addressed a gathering of approximately fifty thousand people on the occasion of Buddha Parinirvana Day. He informed the people that from now on he would devote his life to Buddhism.

Dr Ambedkar discharged his duty as a member of the Rajya Sabha. Then on September 2, 1953, a bill to create Andhra Pradesh was brought. Dr Ambedkar criticised the policy of the government. He said, "Potti Sriramulu had sacrificed his life for principles. Had it happened in some other country, people would have toppled the government."

Those days, Dr Babasaheb's health was precarious. Still, he attended the opening ceremony of Acharya Sadde's new film Mahatma. The ceremony was held on January 4, 1954. The film was based on the life of Mahatma Jyotibarao Phule, whom Dr Ambedkar considered his third guru. His first guru was Lord Buddha and second guru was Kabir Dasji.

In May 1954, a by-election was held for the Bandra seat, which was vacant. Dr Ambedkar contested for it, but he lost by 6,381 votes.

Babasaheb Ambedkar participated in the third 'World Buddhist Brotherhood Conference' held in December 1954 at a place called Kawa, which was 7 kilometres from Rangoon, the capital of Burma.

On May 24, 1956, on the occasion of Gautam Buddha's birthday, he said that he would get initiated in Buddhism in October.

Babasaheb chose October 14, 1956, the day of Vijayadashami, for initiation into Buddhism. On October 11, Baba Saheb left for Nagpur with his wife and his secretary. On reaching Nagpur, he addressed the press and said, "I had promised Gandhiji that I would choose the path which would cause least harm to Hinduism. Buddhism is a sect of Hinduism." Mahathir Chandramani, a Buddhist priest, initiated him and his wife into Buddhism.

It was the morning of October 14, 1956, when Dr Ambedkar underwent the initiation into Buddhism along with his nearly five lakh followers. After this incident, many Dalits converted to Buddhism. Even today, this religious conversion continues among Dalits.

❑

The End

After undergoing initiation, Dr Ambedkar went to Delhi. He visited many Buddhist shrines. Although his health continued to deteriorate he attended the Fourth Buddhist Conference. The conference was held on November 15, 1956 at Sinha Durbar Hall in Kathmandu. He also visited Kushinara on November 30, 1956.

Babasaheb had become old. He was worried that he would die without fulfilling his mission.

Dr Babasaheb was not afraid of death. Once he even told his secretary, Nanakchand Rattu, "I am not afraid of death. I am ready to face it whenever it comes."

On December 4, 1956, Dr Ambedkar briefly attended the Rajya Sabha. Then he had some letters written. On December 5, 1956, he worked all day in his office. In the evening, he asked his secretary Rattu to bring him the typed pages of his book, Buddha and His Dharma. He wanted to work on it at night. Babasaheb could not see the morning of December 6, 1956. When his wife went to his study room at 7:30 in the morning, she saw that Dr Ambedkar had died. She immediately called his secretary and informed his colleagues and cabinet ministers about his death.

Prime Minister Pandit Jawaharlal Nehru and other ministers reached Dr Babasaheb's residence to pay their respects. His body was then taken to Bombay by a special airplane.

The entire Bombay city was shocked to hear this sad news. Thousands of people reached his residence—26, Alipore Road—to pay last respects to their leader. Bombay remained closed on December 7 in his memory.

His last journey began on the afternoon of December 7. Lakhs of people arrived from all over Maharashtra to attend the last journey of their beloved leader. His last rites were performed at Dadar funeral grounds. His pyre was lit by his only son Yashwant Rao. That day, thousands of people declared that they would convert to Buddhism.

Conversion to Buddhism

An era ended with the death of Dr Ambedkar. He was an accomplished politician, but his political acumen had a stamp of scholarship. There was dishonesty at every stage in politics, but he never gave up on truth. He used to proudly say that he had never indulged in dirty politics. He believed in non-violence, but he believed that it should be that like that of a lion. He believed that being deep in a state of sleep could not be called non-violence.

He taught the blind untouchable community to live with self-respect and made it self-supporting. It was a community where an individual lived vulnerably, where he did not even have the normal rights of a common man. He started movements for the benefit of the Dalit community and devoted his whole life to alleviate their suffering.

Even after gaining the highest position, he never kept away from family life. When he stayed in Delhi, he used to sit comfortably on the lawn of his bungalow and eat like a common man.

His gardener would also accompany him during the meal. That he was a common man was reflected in every aspect of his personality. While in Bombay, he slept on a bench on a blanket or sometimes even without it.

Dr Ambedkar's personality was like a storm, which gave many instant earthquake-like shocks to reform Hindu society. Pandit Nehru wrote about him, "Dr Ambedkar was a symbol of rebellion against the oppressive tendencies of Hindu society. Seeing injustice, tyranny and superstition, he used to get angry. Dr Ambedkar, who would assume the form of Chandi on some occasions, used to forget everything the very next moment and laugh out loud. He used to say that one should laugh heartily."

He tried to transform the society by holding equality, freedom and fraternity as the values of life and adopted Buddhism which followed these principles. In short, we can say that the personality of Dr Babasaheb Ambedkar was an ideal personality which was full of human sensibilities and qualities. In his death, we lost a great personality.

❑

Why Did Dr Ambedkar Adopt Buddhism?

People are very curious to know why Ambedkar renounced Hinduism. Ambedkar, who was born in an untouchable family, devoted his whole life to fighting for the eradication of untouchability. During the last days of his life, he renounced Hinduism and adopted Buddhism. What were the reasons for his decision?

We get to know a lot about his decision by reading his book Buddha and His Dharma.

Also, his Annihilation of Caste, Philosophy of Hinduism, Riddles in Hinduism, etc., and his articles, speeches and interviews which he gave before and after converting to Buddhism throw light on this issue.

The 'Yeola Convention' was a historic convention in that respect. Ambedkar believed that the untouchables were considered 'weak and inferior' simply because they were a part of Hindu society. When his concerted efforts failed to get the untouchables the right to equality and to get them 'common rights as human beings', then he thought that it was necessary to adopt another religion—a religion which would give the importance of equality and the right of equality to the untouchables and treat them fairly. He urged his supporters, "Choose that religion which gives you equal importance, equal opportunities and treats you equally."

After deliberating about various religions, Ambedkar came to the conclusion that Buddhism fitted his point of view. In 1950, in his article 'Buddha and the Future of His Religion', published in the journal of the Mahabodhi Society, he expressed his thoughts on religion and Buddhism briefly as follows—

1. To keep society united, there must be either the approval of law or morality. Without them, society would surely crumble to pieces.
2. In order to preserve religion, a harmony of logic has to be brought into it. In other words, this is what is called science.
3. It is not only necessary for any religion to have a code of conduct, but it is also necessary that its code of conduct be based on the fundamental principles of liberty, equality and fraternity.
4. No religion should maintain its purity by making a weapon out of poverty.

Dr Ambedkar was convinced that only Buddhism fulfilled those requirements. Therefore, among all religions, it was the right religion for the world. He felt that a scripture was needed to propagate Buddhism. Therefore, to fulfil the requirement, Dr Ambedkar wrote a book, Buddha and His Dharma.

In this book, Dr Ambedkar has enumerated the evils of Hinduism—

1. It is deprived of moral liberty.
2. It gives importance to the order of conformity.
3. Laws are unfair because they are different for different people. Apart from this, the code itself is considered final.

Dr Ambedkar believed that what is called religion by Hindus is just a pile of orders and prohibitions.

In the same year, in his speech on the occasion of Buddha Jayanti in Delhi, Dr Ambedkar criticised Hindu gods and goddesses and praised Buddhism as he believed it to be based on moral principles. He also said that instead of considering himself as a messenger of God like the promoters of religions, the Buddha called himself only a mentor and gave a revolutionary meaning to the religion. According to Dr Ambedkar, Hinduism shows inequality and Buddhism stands for equality.

In May 1956, Dr Ambedkar delivered a lecture titled 'Why I like Buddhism and why it is beneficial to the world in the current situation'. He delivered this lecture at the British Broadcasting Corporation in London.

He said, "I give priority to Buddhism because of these three principles—Buddhism teaches us prajna (understanding against superstition and supernaturalism), karuna (love) and samata (equality). This is what all people want for a contented and happy life. God and soul cannot save society."

In his speech on May 24, 1956, he spoke about conversion to Buddhism, about adopting it, "Hinduism believes in God. In Buddhism, there is no God. Hindus believe in soul; but according to Buddhism, there is no soul. Hindus believe in casteism, in Chaturvarna. In Buddhism, casteism and Chaturvarna have no place."

Dr Ambedkar considered Buddhism to be more prudent than Hinduism. His main objection to Hinduism was that it accepted inequality and untouchability as righteous and that its four varnas are a proof of that.

On the other hand, Buddhism is fundamentally opposed to Chaturvarna and supports equality. According to him, prajna, samata and karuna alone impart the main teachings of Buddhism that this alone is necessary for a peaceful and contented life.

Eventually, Dr Ambedkar converted to Buddhism. His book, Buddha and His Dharma contains his own understanding and reasoning about Buddhism. In this book, he has also given reasons for conversion to Buddhism and presented rational arguments for Buddhism. He did not believe in God and soul. We can conclude this from the reasons that he gave for adopting Buddhism. In this book, he concludes that there is no place for God and soul in Buddhism. According to Dr Ambedkar, Buddha did not believe in reincarnation nor in karma and moksha as traditionally believed. Buddha also rejected the caste system.

Scholars who have studied Buddhism are convinced that Buddha did not believe in God and soul and that he rejected the varna system. Buddha did not believe in reincarnation and was in favour of nirvana.

Here, Dr Ambedkar's interpretation diverges from the orthodox view of Buddhism. It is not possible to say how he arrived at his interpretation or conclusion.

When Dr Ambedkar accepted Buddhism in 1956, lakhs of people adopted it along with him. They stopped worshipping the gods that they had worshipped for centuries. They also adopted Buddhism as Dr Ambedkar did. There were some people who did not forgive Dr Ambedkar for his betrayal in the form of conversion. Before conversion, the Hindu untouchables believed that Dr Ambedkar gave them self-respect, which they did not expect from Hinduism.

❑

Dalit Politics in India

(After Dr Ambedkar)

Before the birth of the recent Bahujan Samaj Party, the Republican Party of India (RPI) worked for the untouchables in independent India. That was the last political instrument that Dr Ambedkar gave shape to. The Republican Party itself was a modified form of the 'Scheduled Castes Federation'. The party could not achieve success during the elections. It was considered to be an unsuitable organisation for the Buddhists who had broken the shackles of Hindutva. The Independent Labour Party was formed by Ambedkar on the basis of class and not on the basis of caste. When the party was formed, it was beset and faced with many problems.

The first major ideological difference was between those who had their roots in villages, where Mahars were in greater numbers. The second was the youth, who were better educated and ambitious and who lived in the cities. On account of this ideological difference, the RPI was divided into two classes.

After Dr Ambedkar's death, there was no other devoted or committed person working for the social and economic development of Mahars. By 1959, the rift between the two factions of the RPI had become so deep that the two main factions held their separate meetings. In the end, the educated and progressive group of youth from the urban areas was given the responsibility of running the party.

This division of the RPI lasted till the 1962 elections. The party failed to win a single seat for the Lok Sabha from Maharashtra. In the same year, its performance was better in the state assembly. After that, it could win only a few seats in the Maharashtra assembly.

RPI strengthened its roots in Uttar Pradesh owing to Dr Ambedkar's deep influence (especially in the cities of Agra and Aligarh). The party gained unprecedented popularity in Punjab, Haryana, Andhra Pradesh and Karnataka.

The party was more successful in Uttar Pradesh than Maharashtra. The credit for its success in Uttar Pradesh goes to the Buddhist politician B.P. Maurya, who belonged to the Chamar (Jatav) caste. He had organised the untouchables and Muslims. This alliance of sympathy between the Muslims and the untouchables did not last long. The split in the Congress in 1969 completely changed the electoral process in Uttar Pradesh. In 1971, both B.P. Maurya and Ramji Ram who was his fiercest opponent in the party returned to the Lok Sabha, representing Indira Gandhi's Congress Party. Thus, the importance of RPI in Uttar Pradesh came to an end.

In Maharashtra, after Dr Ambedkar's death, one party came to an end and another party emerged.

In 1970, an organisation emerged, which called itself 'Dalit Panther'. It was formed for the downtrodden class and its name 'Dalit Panther' was derived from America's 'Black Panther'. At that time, there was a lack of strong Dalit leaders in India. However, the Dalit Panther also could not establish contact with the Dalits fully as most of the Mahars were still illiterate and were from the villages. Within a few years, this party, like the Republican Party, became a victim of its ideological and personal differences. That ideological difference became especially visible in 1974 when Namdev Dhasal and Raja Dhale appeared as two leaders. It was a historic moment for the 'Dhale faction' when mass Buddhist conversions took place under the leadership of Dr Ambedkar. They would have benefited mainly by spreading Buddhism in the future. On the other hand, Namdev Dhasal was a radical leftist and Marxist. Therefore, he did not give much importance to Dr Ambedkar and his conversion movement. To him, the end of untouchability was the end of the economic plight of a class and not of caste, religion and self-respect. In view of that, Dhasal considered the CPI to be the leader of the Dalits. But within a few years, seeing Indira Gandhi's Garibi Hatao programme during the Emergency, Dhasal was convinced that she was the leader who was really a benefactor of the poor. His party supported the Congress in the 1977 elections.

Till then, 'Dalit Panther' had not been able to decide any main 'role' for itself. The party was active in politics; but without any political party, it did not have any strong programme for herself.

It could not even establish contact with the Mahars, nor could it get in direct contact with the untouchables.

The void that was left by the end of the Panther Party was not filled by any other party or another organisation; surprisingly it was filled by a literary movement.

A whole new anti-apartheid literature emerged. The writers delved thoroughly into the lives of the untouchables for the first time. Some writers were very talented. Dalit literature and its writers became famous and the literature created by them was considered to be a really important contribution.

The emergence of Dalit literature was not confined to Maharashtra; it also emerged in Karnataka on a massive scale. The origin of this movement can be traced back to a speech given by a minister in the Congress government of Karnataka in 1974. Vasalingappa, who belonged to the untouchable caste, considered the language of the state to be Bhapa. He thought that there was a scarcity of literature on the common man and his life in the Kannada language. There are untouchables among the common people as well, who are called 'Adi Karnataka'.

His speech was like a spark falling on a pile of straw, which immediately catches fire. It was both cheered and rebutted. According to staunch Kannada litterateurs, the untouchable minister had defamed Kannada literature by airing such views in his speech. Surprisingly, that speech opened new avenues of writing for the emerging Dalit writers and many Dalit litterateurs. In 1974, a conference of Dalit writers was held, in which thousands of writers participated. Gradually, this Dalit literary movement gained momentum in many directions. For example, a group of young Dalit writers started a popular weekly magazine Sugathi, which emphasised popular culture (film articles) and political and social Dalit dialogues. Its readership was mostly from Adi Karnataka. In 1988, the circulation of this magazine was 65,000 copies.

Without the guidance of Dr Ambedkar, the Dalit literary movement could not establish a solid political platform. The Dalits of Karnataka did not think of forming a Dalit party.

There the Dalit Sangharsh Samiti was formed, which worked for various Dalit organisations in the state. The Dalit activists began awakening consciousness among the children and elders of the Adi Karnataka society. Many Dalit activists adopted Buddhism and studied Buddhist literature.

It is true that the Karnataka movement drew inspiration from Dr Ambedkar's Maharashtra movement. However, some activists opposed reservation in jobs and seats in parliament. They saw reservation as a 'trap' that separated them from the progressive ideology, created a hindrance in working for the benefit of the Dalit society on a large scale and also the representatives of the reserved seats in the Legislative Assembly were viewed with contempt. There was no division in Karnataka on the basis of ideological and philosophical differences; but tensions cropped up in Maharashtra over the Dr Ambedkar's movement, which had a disastrous effect on the movement.

The Dalit movement in Karnataka remained confined to the cities. The Dalits in villages in Karnataka were not included in the movement, where the main need of the Dalits was literacy and cultural and religious development. The movement did not gain momentum in the villages of Karnataka and Maharashtra.

In Bihar, there was a wave of revolution due to this movement, which gave birth to Marxist ideology. That should not lead to the conclusion that Marxist ideology was the right ideology, which is helpful for the development of Dalits or that the principles of Dr Ambedkar are less helpful in the development of rural India. We can see that Kanshi Ram has worked for the welfare and development of rural and urban Dalits in Uttar Pradesh, guided by Dr Ambedkar's thoughts.

In Bihar, the movement gained momentum only owing to some primary issues, such as—social respect, land rights and rise in remuneration. These are the issues which have a direct bearing on the progress of the untouchables. Such themes were at the core of Dr Ambedkar's 'Independent Labour Party'. The same principles were also followed by the later-formed 'Republican Party' and 'Dalit Panther' to some extent. But not all the parties worked on these programmes to their full potential. After independence, these organisations were cut off every day from the Mahars of the village. Similarly, apart from Mahars, they also lost touch with the other communities.

To an extent, Buddhism also intervened in these problems. In spite of possessing the potential for personal empowerment, Buddhism did not raise its voice for the immediate problems of the Mahars or the problems of other rural untouchables.

So far, under the Dalit leadership of Maharashtra, plans have been made for the advancement of uneducated untouchables in the villages on the basis of Buddhism. But unfortunately, the gap between Mahar Buddhists and other poor Hindus is increasing.

But in spite of all these limitations, the movement started by Dr Ambedkar became a powerful medium for bringing about dynamism and awakening consciousness in western India. Babasaheb's thoughts and philosophy of life came to the fore in the form of development and progress in other parts of the country as well.

Demonstrations and protests were held in Maharashtra itself regarding the re-publishing of Riddles in Hinduism, a book containing a compilation of articles by Babasaheb Ambedkar. The Maharashtra government and Dalit scholars could not agree on its publication or republication.

Even when Dr Ambedkar was alive, the articles were considered provocative and even after his death, the situation remains the same. This book is still considered controversial.

Today, the views of Babasaheb Ambedkar are taken seriously only in Maharashtra and Karnataka; in the rest of the country, he is found only in the form of posters and statues.

Today, Babasaheb has remained only a reflection among his disciples and politicians, from which people want to say that they are fighting for their caste and community.

Instead of improving the image of Dalits, today in the twenty-first century, people are busy improving their image. Today, Gandhiji's image has suffered the biggest blow. Gandhiji, once considered a well-wisher of the Harijans, is today being rejected by the Dalits or his views are being disregarded.

Today, Dr Ambedkar's thoughts are lighting thousands of paths for development and Dalit progress just as he guided thousands of people during his lifetime.

❑

Inspirational Thoughts of Bhimrao Ambedkar

- The individual is made by society. Though this is a very general and prosaic statement, it is very strong. Society is never made of individuals; it is made of class. Classes exist in every society. The reasons underlying the creation of class are different. Sometimes classes are formed due to economic reasons and at other times due to intellectual and political reasons.
- One wants to live as a unit of some class or the other. This is a universal truth. Hindu

society is no exception to this. According to this rule, classes got transformed into castes. In fact, caste and class are like neighbours living opposite each other. Their existence seems to be different because of very minor differences. In fact, caste itself is a limited class.

- It is possible that I may be wrong, but I have always felt that it is better to make mistakes than to follow the guidance and orders of others and sit silently and spoil or ruin the situation.
- Scholars more qualified than myself have tried to unravel the mysteries of caste. But it is a pity that it is not yet explained and we have minimal knowledge about it. I am aware of the complexity of institutions like caste and I am not so pessimistic that the puzzle is incomprehensible and unfathomable because I believe it can be understood. The problem of caste is a formidable problem, both theoretically and practically.
- No matter how much Indian society talks about the purity of blood, it is not a pure-

blooded society. In Indian society, there is a mixture of Aryans, Dravidians, Mongols, Shakas, Huns, Abhiras, Nagas, Yakshas, etc. Many castes travelling from other countries came here, settled down and got assimilated in the cultural stream of this country. These castes became the mantra of this country by pushing away their predecessors. Due to their constant communication and relations, an integrated culture was born.

- It is illogical to say that Indian society is a compilation of different castes. Compilation does not create homogeneity. If seen from the point of view of difference in blood, then Indian society is heterogeneous. Yes, this compilation is culturally very dense. On this basis, I say that there is no other country in the world except this peninsula, which has so much cultural harmony. We are not only united in material terms, but our cultural unity is also unceasing and indestructible, which is spread in all four directions throughout the country. Due to this cultural homogeneity, the caste system has become so formidable that it is difficult to explain it. It is a difficult task because there is infiltration of the caste system even in a homogeneous society.

- We can never understand the problems of the Indian caste system from the perspective of the principles of European anthropology and sociology. The caste system in India refers to the division of society into artificial parts, bound by differences in customs and marriages. The result is clear that endogamy is the only goal that characterises the caste system, and if we are able to find out why endogamous marriages take place, we can practically prove how castes originated and what is their structure.
- Which was the first class which transformed into caste? In other words, who should be called the originator of the caste system? Initially, the Brahmin class turned into a caste. This Brahmin class encouraged the caste system in the country.

- Manu is not the originator of the caste system. The caste system existed hundreds of years before Manu. Manu elevated this system to a philosophical plane and gave it a scientific form. Manu has only compiled the rules related to caste.
- Unequal social structure cannot end with sentimentality or ideals. It requires a changed mindset and concrete programmes.
- Till date (till 1935), all the agitations occurred only to resolve family issues. There was no discussion of restructuring the entire society. Reforms like widow marriage, old-age marriage, child marriage, etc., are associated with the individual and the family and not with the social structure. The upper castes were more interested in family reforms. Their interests were protected that way. They did not feel the need to confront caste or class distinctions. They could not understand the pain of a society that was neglected due to caste and class. The problems related to

women such as widow marriage and old-age marriage were more severe in their own class, due to which their social reforms were confined to their class. A vision that there should be a change in the social structure emerged only after the British arrived on the scene.

- The caste institution is not only a division of labour, it is also a division of labourers. It does not stop only by dividing the labourers, but it keeps each group of labourers above each other from bottom to top—and the worst part is that this hierarchy is forever stuck on the basis of birth. In no other country in the world has the division of labour been aligned with the social status of the labourers.
- Indian society is made up of such a ladder-like sequence, in which the man at the top of the ladder despises or looks down on the man at the bottom, and the man at the bottom looks with respect at the man at the top. In such a society, there is not even the slightest scope for equality, fraternity and democracy to flourish.

How can there be inequality, discrimination, anger and hatred in a democracy?

- Can we get rid of the flaws which entered the Hindu society due to the caste system? How can the caste system be destroyed? It is believed that to destroy the caste system, first of all, sub-castes should be destroyed, which is wrong. In this effort, the castes will become stronger, more powerful and deeply entrenched.
- Inter-caste marriage is the only way to break the caste system. The feeling of intimacy is created only because of blood relations. For this reason, if inter-caste marriages become more common, the bonds of caste will weaken. There will be more closeness towards each other.
- The caste system is man-made. It can be demolished. Caste is an imaginary system, a mental state. Changing one's mindset is not an easy task.
- Hindus follow the caste system. The only reason for this is that Hindus are basically religious. Caste has been linked to religiosity.

The original religion itself has supported a wrong inhuman system. This system cannot be demolished by making fun of the scriptures. To counter it, there is an urgent need for intense rationalism and commitment to egalitarian social-building.

- At the root of the conduct of the people attached to caste and varna are the beliefs that have continued for thousands of years.
- Raising the slogan of inter-caste marriage will not work. The new system alone is not going to work.
- Whenever the ideal and imaginary varna system is propagated, then the common man gets a major reason to stick to the caste.
- There is a need to strike at the roots of the caste system itself. Unless the roots are broken, the mentality of untouchability cannot be eradicated. The attempt to find the basis in the scriptures to destroy untouchability and caste discrimination is in fact a ridiculous attempt to clean the mud with mud.

- To me, this Chaturvarnya, in which the old names have been retained, is an abomination against which my nature rebels. But I do not wish to object to Chaturvarnya merely on the basis of feelings. I have a solid reason to oppose it. After a thorough examination of this ideal, I am fully convinced that Chaturvarnya as a system of social organisation has been impractical, fatal and utterly unsuccessful. From the practical point of view too, many such difficulties arise from Chaturvarnya, which its supporters did not pay attention to.
- The basic principle of caste is different from that of varna; it is not only fundamentally different, but it is also fundamentally conflicting.
- What will you do if a person has attained high status not on the basis of merit but on the basis of birth? How will you handle it? The answer is that you have to abolish the caste system.
- Plato divided people into three categories on the basis of nature. But what happened? He

failed. The principle of Chaturvarnya is against human nature. It cannot be implemented even if the policy of penal-legislation is applied to make it mandatory.

- The ideal human society is one which is founded on the spirit of equality, liberty and fraternity and whose foundation is laid on renunciation, sacrifice, dedication, truth, non-violence and love. If this is not the case in a society, how can it be called a society? Society is man-made and it was created for the convenience and development of everyone.
- Seeing your sad face and hearing your despairing voice, my heart is torn. You have been suffering atrocities for so long and yet the thought of giving up timidity and superstition does not cross your mind. Why don't you die the moment you are born? Why do you burden the earth with your pathetic, disgusting and neglected life? If you cannot adopt a new life and cannot change your situation, then it is far better to die than to

live like this. Surely, it is your birthright to have food, clothing and shelter. If you want to live with dignity, then you must believe in self-help because that is the best help.

- Only when Hindu society becomes a unilateral society it will build the power to protect itself. In the absence of this inner strength, Swaraj will prove to be a ladder to slavery, not a ladder to freedom.
- Even if we accept that Chaturvarnya is practical, I will say with certainty that it is a very flawed system wherein a Brahmin should promote education, a Vaishya should do business and a Shudra should serve others. Although it was meant for division of labour, was the purpose of this model that Shudras should not acquire wealth, etc? This is a very interesting question. The proponents of Chaturvarnya draw a conclusion as to why a Shudra should take the trouble of acquiring wealth, etc., when all three varnas are there to assist him. If a Shudra needs to read and

write, he can go to a Brahmin. Why should Shudras worry about carrying weapons, when Kshatriyas are there? According to this kind of understanding of the Chaturvarnya principle, it can be said that a Shudra is dependent and the three varnas are his protectors.

- Each person should receive education; everyone should have means of defence. These are the ultimate requirements of every individual for contemplation. What help can an uneducated and disarmed person get from his neighbour who is educated and armed?
- There is no doubt that in practice the relationship of Chaturvarnya was actually that of a master and a servant. The relations between Brahmins, Kshatriyas and Vaishyas were also not pleasant, but they managed to work together. The Brahmins pleased the Kshatriyas and both allowed the Vaishyas to survive so that they could survive with his support. But all three agreed to demote the Shudra. He was not allowed to acquire wealth lest he should not remain dependent

on the three classes. He was prevented from acquiring education lest he should become aware of his welfare. It was forbidden for him to bear arms lest he should acquire the means to rebel against their authority.

- The root of our thinking should be 'man'. It is our moral responsibility to make available to man his human rights. The scriptures took away human rights, so it is necessary to refute them.
- Religion is for man; man is not for religion.
- As long as the untouchables remain in Hindu society, their standard of living will not improve and they will continue to be exploited, humiliated and destitute. An untouchable's fate will never change. Anyone will convert him to his religion by giving him financial inducements. As a result, there would never be any revolution in Hindu society. It will rot in the darkness of dogmas. If you want to live in Hindu society, the standard of living will not improve without making revolutionary changes in it.

- The economic condition of the untouchables is deteriorating everyday. They do not have social harmony, the hold on cohabitation and status. Yet how has it remained the unit of Hindu society? No class can live with dignity in a society without getting social respect. All this is not possible without bringing about a social revolution.
- I have objection to Gandhiji's term 'Harijan', the main points of which are as follows—
  1. Will the untouchable not remain untouchable by becoming a Harijan?
  2. Won't he pick up dirt or sweep?
  3. Will this enable other varnas to embrace him?
  4. Will Hindu society stop considering him as an untouchable and accept him as a savarna?
  5. Will this give him the right to social equality?
- If not, then why create the trap of Harijan? What is the use of that path by which the self-respect of the untouchables cannot be restored? Everyone is a Harijan.

- No man can be thankful after being humiliated, no woman can be thankful when her modesty is violated and no nation can be thankful for losing its independence. Then how can an untouchable thank Gandhiji after being humiliated by the usage of the word 'Harijan'?
- As long as the untouchable class is a part of Hindu society, it will not progress. They should renounce Hindu society to get true freedom. This will give them freedom to don clothes, eat and drink, work, get education, live in a cultured society, etc.
- You have nothing to lose. You will only lose your shackles. You will acquire many benefits after conversion. If we look at the problem of conversion from the social point of view, then on the surface, this struggle may appear for achieving social prestige, yet it is often a class struggle. The oppression by the superior classes is only a part of the constant struggle between the entitled and the unemployed. The untouchables lack three essential powers

for the struggle to be fruitful. Those powers are human power, material power and intellectual power. As long as you remain in Hindu society, you will be unable to get these three powers.

- Some people ask—what are you going to gain by converting? The answer to that is—what will India gain from independence? The untouchables need conversion as much as India needs Swaraj. The ultimate purpose of conversion and Swaraj is freedom.
- There should be a uniform civil law. Where there are differences of opinion in laws based on Hindu, Muslim and Christian religions, they should be resolved thoughtfully. There are also some common issues in all of them. Only the contentious issues cannot be resolved. Uniform civil law is our ultimate aim.
- Dalits have to play an important and pivotal role in the fight for social equality. The weaker sections should organise themselves and acquire their rights. I am trying to get

the untouchable society its political rights. There are many youths working for the independence of the country. The Dalit youth have to emancipate themselves. True independence is possible only with the emancipation of Dalits.

- The facilities of education should reach the most exploited and neglected people of the society. There should be a system wherein the class that has been traditionally neglected should not have to spend more for higher education. Colleges and universities need to come together to enable cultural progress of graduates and students through the curriculum.
- Education is like a double-edged weapon. An educated person who is characterless and immodest is worse than an animal. If the knowledge and education of a well-educated person goes against the public interest, then such a person proves to be a curse for society.
- There is no caste distinction between untouchables and upper castes. Earlier

this difference was between the victor and conquered. Like race discrimination, business discrimination is also not its basis.

- Chandalas and untouchables are not synonyms. They are different. The class of Chandalas originated in the period of the Dharma Sutras, but the class of untouchables was created many years later, around 400 BC.
- Why do the untouchables live outside the village all over the country? In primitive times, there used to be constant battles between the gangs. When those groups were transformed into a permanent society, then people from the displaced groups from other places came over to them. They were not allowed inside the village and had to live outside the village. The displaced had to stay outside the village not only in India but in many countries of the world.
- In the Aryan-Dravidian conflict, the victorious Aryans conquered the Dravidians and made them Shudras. Before this, the Dravidians had conquered the tribals and made them

untouchables. Dravidians and Nagas prove both of them to be of the same lineage. Later, the Aryans displaced the Naga people and declared them untouchables.

- If genetic anatomy is the basis for determining different races, then if we evaluate the different castes of Hindu society (based on head, eyes, nose, chin, complexion, stature, etc.), then it will be proved that untouchables, Aryans and the Dravidian lineages are not different from each other. The measurement of different parts of the body will prove that Brahmins and the untouchables are people of the same lineage. If Brahmins are Aryans, then untouchables are also Aryans.
- The untouchables were Buddhists. When Shankaracharya restored Hinduism at the philosophical level, a large section of society returned to Hinduism owing to authority, power and terror. But there was a section which was not prepared to give up Buddhism. Those people were despised and

made untouchable. This conspiracy started two thousand five hundred years ago.

- Religion is life and life is religion. For example, human contemplation on what is life has gone on incessantly and it will continue in the future, too. Similarly, thinking about religion will never stop. Today, where there is religion, there are conflicts about religion. These conflicts are not taking place today, rather they have been going on for centuries.
- There is no religion on this earth which has not gone through the phase of rise and fall. There is not even the slightest opposition to the humanistic approach in any religion. Nevertheless, there have been frequent crusades and religion has taken the form of adharma, leaving its innate nature. Thousands of stories will be found in the history of religion as to how religion remains religion even after becoming adharma. The reasons will also be known. Yet religion will continue to repeat this history.

- Religion is one of the most powerful driving forces in human history and its worth can only be understood in the light of the social ideal it represents. Every religion should be judged by justice and utility. Religion is another name for justice, liberation, equality and fraternity.
- The root of the disparity between religion and society is the Chaturvarnya system. Chaturvarnya is the mother of untouchability. Caste discrimination and untouchability are other forms of inequality. If this root is not destroyed, then the untouchable class will certainly give up this religion.
- There is no dearth of people who saddened by the pathetic condition of the untouchables, lighten the burden on their hearts by declaring that they should do something for the untouchables. But among those who want to solve this problem, there is hardly anyone who says that we should also do something to transform the touchable Hindus. The belief

persists that if anyone needs reform, it is the untouchables. If anything has to be done, it has to be done for the untouchables, and if the untouchables are reformed, then the feeling of untouchability will disappear.

- The caste system makes man insensitive. It is a process of sterility. Education, property and labour are necessary for every person who wants to attain free and full humanity. The backwardness and inaction of society can be mainly blamed on the unnatural and unscientific social system.
- Can anyone believe that there is an animal called man, whose mere touch makes water dirty, man corrupt and God unworthy of worship? If there is such a man, he is an untouchable, who is considered worse than an animal in Hinduism and Hindu society.
- If everyone does not have equal rights in a religion, then does that religion remain a religion?
- If the Hindu society becomes a homochromatic society, then only it will have the power to protect itself. In the absence of this inner

strength, independence will be a ladder to slavery and not a ladder to freedom for the Hindus.

- I see religious philosophy as the natural religious philosophy, in which the existence of God is inseparably bound with nature. There are three bases of religious philosophy—
    - (a) God rules and he is the creator of Nature, which we call the world.
    - (b) God is the regulator of the world, i.e. he is the controller and
    - (c) God imposes his authority on humanity through morality.
- Religion is not the subject of any descriptive or scientific analysis. The religious philosophy is analytical philosophy as long as it does not contain logic in itself. But once logic is incorporated, it becomes standard scientific content.
- I do not think that all religious philosophies will have one philosophy, rather there is something different in all religions. Any

movement or organisation has a revolutionary philosophy, on the basis of which that organisation operates.

- In ancient society, man recognised his political God as everything. Modern society recognises the human aspect, which excludes God from society, yet accepts God.
- In ancient society, there was a god for each community. There was no integrated and universal God as in modern society. It thought of humanity as a collective. He only thought about his community, which is not the case at present.
- An emergence of a revolution brings a state of dispassionateness in life and leads life in that direction where the authority of religion succeeds. In the second one, the 'real rule' of religious thought is established, which has the concept of creation of good humanity by divine power. This system is about transformation.

- Although the entire society in the whole world is not entirely made up of a single class and every society has classes, yet the classes in other societies are fundamentally different.
- There are four reasons for the need of a religion in the life of a person—
    1. Morals are needed for stability and control of society. In the absence of any one of these, the society can go to the abyss. That is why a society needs religion.
    2. He must be a rationalist to maintain religion. Science is rationalist.
    3. Mere code of ethics does not mean religion. The ethics of religion should recognise the basic principles of liberty, equality and fraternity.
    4. No religion should insist on accepting poverty as sacred or glorify poverty.
- Initially there were four varnas. The basis of varnas was religion and later these four varnas became castes. The four varnas were

divisions of the same part. It was not division of work but that of labour. Casteism has originated from this religion. It has confined a person to his caste. Due to this, the qualities of human beings have become secondary. Where there is caste, there is no purity.

- Religion is a personal matter of the liberation of the human soul.
- Religion maintains mutual harmony and morality of human beings on the basis of morals.
- Religion is the path of the identification of the mind, soul and purification.
- The foundation of religion should be laid on virtue and pure conduct.
- Religion should be articulated by behaviour, not by religious texts.
- Religion does not accept discrimination.
- Religion is another name for compassion, love and sacrifice. Religion conquers hatred with love and it rules the hearts of people without being a ruler.

- Religion is the nectar that provides peace to the disturbed mind. He who follows religion is in love and treats everyone equally.
- Religion is supportive to the helpless, the dumb and the handicapped. That is their indelible power.
- They claim religion to be immutable. The foundation of all religions is faith. To receive God's grace and to be saved by his mercy is the path of religion. Apart from this, everything else is considered unrighteous and prohibited. Apart from God and faith, the facts have no place in religion. No religion has recognised man's intellect, his thoughts, etc. For this reason, the existence of God cannot be discussed at all.
- The religion spoken about by a man named Siddhartha is beyond the prevailing weaknesses. This is a religion which was told or professed by one person to many people. Esotericism has no place in this religion. Divine grace, boon or curse, heaven or hell—

there is no scope for these in this religion. Siddhartha's religion has been propagated in the words, in the language of and for the people of flesh and blood like him. There is no place for faith in this religion. On the contrary, it urges one not to have blind faith in any person or thing. Ask questions, raise doubts, ponder and accept only if it is accepted by the conscience—this is the insistence of this religion. Siddhartha does not claim to be omniscient anywhere. He doesn't talk about giving messages to anyone. In fact, he doesn't give any orders, he doesn't refer to anything that is conclusive. That is the power of this religion.

- A true religion proclaims and establishes equal opportunities; all other religions are false, drivel and pretentious.
- My followers, after me, Buddhism will be administrated by you. If you cannot assimilate it, how will you follow it? Religion accepts mental purity in your conduct.

- Religion seeks to build moral character on the basis of liberty, equality, fraternity and only Buddhism talks of equal opportunities for humanity.
- If we look at the problem of conversion from a spiritual point of view, then it can be said that personal development is the aim of true religion. I accept that definition of religion which pertains to all the people. For that, religion should teach virtues of fraternity, equality and liberty.
- On account of untouchability, your virtues proved to be fruitless. Because of untouchability, you do not get entry in the army, in the police department or in the navy. Untouchability is a curse for you and has deprived you of the right life, respect and prestige in the world. For the untouchables, there is a need for social freedom rather than legal freedom.
- Talking about conversion is not child's play. Just as a rower rows a boat by estimating the

number of passengers and then takes care of the rest of his belongings, we have to work in the same way.

- When the Dhigha Nikaya try to write a biography of Lord Buddha on the basis of Pali texts, then we have a problem and coherent and scientific expression of the teachings in them becomes very difficult. The reality is that among all the religious founders in the world, the discussion or description of Lord Buddha brings to us many such problems, the solutions for which is difficult if not impossible.
- Buddha's Dhamma is not about the other world. It is only related to this world. It talks about neither heaven nor hell; it talks about the earth. This Dhamma does not talk about individual salvation, it gives the message of social liberation. This Dhamma is atheist, materialistic, materialistic and rationalist. This Dhamma is not immutable, transmutation is part of it. This religion is considerate.

- Compared to other religions, Buddhism proves to be superior on the basis of modern, scientific findings and criteria. It accepts the challenges of the modern era. This Dhamma can be verified in the light of modern values like rationalism, social authority, fraternity, freedom, socialism, democracy, etc.
- There is no place for the theoretical proof, bookish proof anywhere in Buddha's thought-system and logic. Buddha's logic stands on direct evidence and conjecture. Buddha once said, "Don't take my words as proof. Accept that as truth which suits your intellect or experience. Nothing is final and unchangeable in this world. Change and continuous change—that is the truth."
- Buddha's Dhamma is social, not people-centric. Buddhist philosophy does not come under the word 'religion'. It is Dhamma or philosophy of religion. Buddhism gave utmost importance to morality. This morality alone is the Dhamma. Without it, the concept of society is not possible. This morality should

be for the promotion of liberty, equality and fraternity.

- We are prepared to lay down our lives for the religion that cares for us, gives us opportunities. Why should we care about a religion that doesn't care for us?
- The society can choose both religion and magistrate—religion should be there where society follows religion and a magistrate where it does not.
- Religion is for man's own humanity. He should not be made a scapegoat for the development of religion.
- There can be no compromise against the principle and it should not even be.
- Parents only give birth to the child; they do not give him the future. The future can only be made by him.
- All the poor, downtrodden and under privileged people in India are silently enduring poverty as punishment from God. They do not consider it as a disease of society

and economy. They will endure exploitation, injustice, torture and rape, but they will not go to court.

- The British are exploiting Indians by taking advantage of the rupee and pound relations. India cannot benefit from currency exchange. It should not be implemented due to lack of domestic stability of gold standard.
- I was born to take responsibility of common people. I was born in a poor family and grew up like poor people in the Improvement Trust chawl in Bombay. I know your complaints. The shell system is exploiting your blood. The method of shelling should end. When this happens, you will find peace and prosperity. You should continue this movement till you achieve your goal.
- Mahars are the most prominent untouchable caste of Maharashtra. The following facts

define the rights of Mahars and touchable Hindus—

1. Mahars are found in every village.
2. All the villages of Maharashtra are surrounded by walls. The Mahars have to guard them in turn.
3. The Mahars also had some rights, including the right to the land.

- It was an old custom of Mahars to own watan lands, which was confirmed by Hindu–Muslim inscriptions. But the British Government imposed a huge tax on this land, due to which the troubles of the Mahars increased greatly.
- Due to the cruel watan system, the Mahar caste regressed towards slavery.
- The Watan system should be abolished, i. e. in every village, the Mahars who are enslaved by Hindus, should be freed like other citizens. The ancestral service performed by the Mahars should be conditional. The Mahars

should be given ownership rights by treating the land as permanent land.

- Although the work, service, timing and remuneration of the watandars were uncertain, the watandars should be treated as government servants. Entire families of watandars were compelled to serve not only the government but also the village officials and the Patil and Kulkarni at any given time. Since the watandars had to satisfy the ranks above themselves who were free to grab land, there was no security for their homeland.
- History is not always a quote, rather it is often a warning, too.
- Firstly, the labour code is not a burden; secondly, due to its existence, it is possible to develop an equitable relationship between the employer and the worker. This is the actual stage when the labour law should be implemented.
- Everyone should get opportunities. It will never be possible to devise a public formula

for everybody to be equal. Changes will always occur according to the needs and strength.

- A democratic society cannot be averse to mechanisation. The slogan of modern civilisation is the machine. Evil has not arisen because of machines or because of modern civilisation. It is a by-product of the wrong social structure.
- It is the firm view of our party that fragmenting the agricultural land and placing the burden of the increasing population on it are the reasons for the poverty of the farmers in the true sense. Reviving old businesses and starting new ones are the only corrective measures. To increase the production power and efficiency of the people, we are going to undertake a comprehensive programme of starting businesses related to technical education and where required, businesses owned and controlled by the government.
- The tenant farmers should be protected from the exploitation by the owners. The tenant

farmers were assured of safety so that the owners would not drive them away. Laws will be formed in the interest of labourers. Laws should be made to provide jobs, for dismissal, to give bonuses in factories, to fix working hours, to give leave, to arrange accommodation, etc. Land will be given to the landless to get rid of unemployment.

- Industrial peace cannot be realised through power. Industrial peace can be attempted through legislation but cannot be guaranteed. If social justice is made the basis of industrial peace, then its results can be quite favourable, because social justice considers the interests of both the owner and the worker. The fight is only about the fact that the owner wants to earn maximum profit by giving minimum wages to the worker and the worker wants proper remuneration for his living. The attitude of the employer is capitalist and that of the worker is always socialist. When capitalism tries to swallow labour or socialism, then the owner and the worker come face to face. As a result of exploitation of labour, the worker has to face not only economic inequalities but also mental agonies which leads to unrest taking the form of strikes. After all, why doesn't the capitalist think that both he and the worker are social animals and production is the result of the combined efforts of both? Labour is also capital. Why does he want to deny labour capital?

- As a teenager, I used to deliver tiffin to my relatives. So, I have some knowledge about labour problems. Now we have started to overcome economic difficulties. Till now, we Dalits used to gather as untouchables, today we are together as labourers.
- The opportunities that the Dalits get are very limited. There are many occasions where they do not get opportunities because of untouchability. The untouchables are not employed in certain departments of the textile mills. In railways, they rot as gangmen and can't even become porters. So long as

injustice and partiality openly exist, how is labour unity possible without their defeat?

- Strike is a civil offence, not a criminal offence. To make man work against his will is slavery.
- If the Congress had called for British imperialism, I would have cooperated with the party, but that was not the reality. The Congress Party is implementing the constitutional government system which it has been handed over only for the welfare of the capitalists and people who are constantly involved in self-interest. It has sacrificed the welfare of farmers and labourers.
- If inflation and internal price-imbalance are to be removed, the mint should be closed. The value of gold should be benchmarked for flexibility in currency.
- Land is the only source of income for the country today; so, those who hold onto a lot of land like parasites and get a lot of income from it must pay income tax.
- The elite of any caste or community play a key role in the progress of their caste and

community; since their powers are wide, they can help the people of their class. They are also expected to be instrumental in the progress of their community. The Dalit elite cannot be an exception to this. Since the elite are recognised and respected members in their respective fields, Dalits expect that the elite will prove to be helpful in their development.

- Self-governance is not enough, rather a good government which is committed to the development of all sections of society is needed.
- Self-governance alone cannot be considered complete, whereas the Congress demands self-governance. Freedom will be considered complete when every citizen of the society experiences this freedom and participates equally in government and non-government establishments.
- Just as independence is the birthright of Brahmins, so is it of Mahars. Anyone will

accept this. Therefore, it is the first duty of the upper class to educate the Dalits and try to raise their morale and social status. Unless this happens, the day of India's independence will be far away—there is no doubt about it.

- It is not as if everything will become possible only after India becomes independent. India should become a nation in which every citizen has equal religious, social, economic and political rights and everyone gets a fair and equal opportunity for the development of personality.
- The political idealism of the majority will become the idealism of the society.
- Democracy is a way of leading public life. Democracy is a system by which revolutionary changes can be brought about in the economic and social sphere without shedding a drop of blood.
- If the power remains secure in the hands of one person or only one political party, then the parliamentary system and democracy are destroyed in that nation and a state of anarchy

arises. A strong opposition party will control the ruling party and try to steer it towards the larger public interest.

- The elite has a significant hold on Indian politics and it is no longer centred on public welfare. This will not benefit the entire society, farmers and labourers.
- There are only two classes in the world—poor and rich, exploited and exploiter. Another is the middle class, which is really small. Farmers and labourers are exploited and that is why they need to be organised.
- All Indians should get equal treatment.
- There should be such a system in all areas of life whereby each person can develop on the strength of his intelligence and talent.
- Every Indian should get economic, religious and political freedom.
- Every Indian should get equal opportunities.
- May every Indian be free from his own needs and fears. It is the responsibility of the state to keep him free from these two.
- One person should not exploit another person, one varna should not exploit another

varna, one nation should not exploit another nation.

- I don't like it when some people say that we are Indians first and then Hindus and Muslims. I do not accept this. Allegiance to Indianness cannot flourish in the midst of competing allegiance of religion, culture, language, etc. I want people to be Indians first and to be Indians till the end. Nothing but Indians.
- And I say with full force in this House that whenever there is a conflict between the interest of the country and the interest of the untouchables, I will give priority to the interest of the untouchables. If any militant majority speaks in the name of the country, I will not support it. I will not support any party just because that party speaks in the name of the country. All those who are present and those who are not present must understand my stand. If there is a conflict between my own interest and the interest of the country, then I will give preference to the country. But if there is a conflict between the interests of the

country and the interests of the Dalits, then I will give priority to the interests of the Dalits.

- Change in the status of Dalits is necessary for the establishment of an egalitarian society. The caste system is not only against human dignity but also against the dream of an egalitarian society.
- The caste system existed even before Manu. Therefore, it is a mistake to say that the caste categories were created by the Shastras and Smritis.
- No other country can compete with India in terms of cultural unity. It has not only a geographical unity but also a deeper and more fundamental unity which is cultural unity, which pervades the whole country from one end to the other. But it is because of this cultural homogeneity that it becomes very difficult to solve the problem of caste.
- Social revolution is needed to break the caste system. Social reforms are not enough.
- In the present system of European society, wealth is the main source of power. But

this idea is a ruse. Religious–philosophical ideologies have played a seminal role in the context of India and Indian Marxists have been unable to understand this part.

- It is worth mentioning in what form the religion of Manu has now remained. It has to be acknowledged that Manu's Dharma has had no enforceable power in the form of law, in the form of rules which are binding on a court to adjudicate disputes. Exceptions to this are matters like marriage, succession, etc., which affect only the individual. It cannot be enforced as a law regulating social conduct and civil rights. But even though it is no longer recognised as a law, it still exists as a practice. Compared to the law, customs are also not insignificant. It is true that the law is enforced by the state through its police force and the practice cannot be enforced by the state if it is not valid. But in practice, this difference is of no importance. The masses enforce customs with the same power with which the state enforces the law. The reason for this is that the binding power of the organised masses is much stronger than the binding power of the state. Technically, Manu's religion has not been a law, yet this has not affected its convertibility.

- Corruption is harmful to the parliamentary democratic system. Democracy will be destroyed if corruption increases.
- My political goal is—
    1. To enable the downtrodden and disadvantaged to get political rights.
    2. While maintaining political, social and economic balance, to give the basis of democracy to the people in these areas.
    3. Organisation of the labour front without distinction of caste and religion.
    4. To give an impression of people's power through political power.
    5. To achieve the goal of being educated, organised and struggler.
- The democratic system is a changing system.
- Only when the following elements are present

in the social structure of a country that the success of democracy is possible—

1. There should not be a lot of inequality in that social system.
2. There should be existence of an opposition party.
3. There should be equality in law and administration. They are complementary and not antagonistic to each other.
4. The people and the government should have the spirit to follow the constitutional morality. The conduct should not be unconstitutional.
5. The domination by the majority is not accepted.
6. In that society, moral values are given paramount importance. Moral values are determined by conduct.
7. There should be an awakened public opinion and should be sensitive to the administration of the country. They should have great awareness about the

happenings in the country and laws that are passed.

- Social structure based on class has always proved to be a threat to democracy because on one hand, in the class-based society, there are oppression, lies, arrogance, greed and selfishness and on the other hand, there is complete lack of freedom, identity, self-respect and prestige. Insecurity, poverty and fear also exist in such a society.
- Laws are made for people by people. There is a need for continuous amendment in the law, but this amendment should also be done with the consent of all. There should be one law for all in all places. In it, everyone's interest is protected. Law should be social and human, i.e. its effect should be universal. The importance of law should be proved through education, it should be disseminated. But the public should not look at the law with fear.

Law should be based on five human values—

1. Law is for the benefit of the people.
2. Law is unfettered or free from the source of fear.
3. Law is secular.
4. It is human-inspired rather than God-inspired.
5. It is amendable as per requirement.

- Equality in politics and inequality in the economic field—this scene needs to be changed. The gap between the two needs to be bridged very quickly. If it does not happen in the near future, then such classes languishing in inequality will expose the mask of democracy.
- Although the government realised that the zamindars were exploiting and sucking the blood of the helpless, poor and downtrodden it did not put an end to these evil acts that made the lives of the Dalits miserable for centuries. The government has the legal power to end

these evils, but it has not changed the present code of social life.

- We were untouchables before the British Government. Has the British Government done anything to end it? Before the British Government, we could not draw water from wells. Has the British Government given us this right? Before the British Government, we did not have the right to enter the temple, police and army. Has this government given us that right? Even though 150 years have passed since the British rule in India, the condition of the untouchables has remained the same.
- Those who study Buddhist history in India know that the people who started propagating Buddhism were the Naga people. The Nagas were Non-Aryans. There was great enmity between the Aryans and the Nagas. Many wars were fought between Aryans and Non-Aryans. The Aryans wanted to destroy the Non-Aryans completely. Many stories will be found in the Puranas related to this. The

Aryans burnt down the Nagas. Sage Agastya saved one Naga and we are believed to be the descendants of that Naga.

- Our goal is not just to get water and enter the temple, but to go beyond it and achieve egalitarianism. Our goal is to destroy the varna system, due to which inequality has risen in society.
- The basis of Hinduism is the varna system, which makes us untouchables. I do not accept the caste system and untouchability of the Hindu system. I do not accept any authority other than the Bhagavad Gita. Although I do not accept the authority of the Vedas, I am a Sanatana Hindu.
- The success or failure of any work depends as much on the means as on its moral nature. If truth lies at the root of the work, there is no need to worry about the result because will-power is needed in the satyagrahis. The work which brings people together is good work. This is our ideology. We have taken it from the Gita. Satyagraha is the main proposition

of the Gita. The Gita is acceptable to both the touchable and the untouchable. The basis of our movement is bringing people together.

- A person's fight for truth or non-truth does not depend on the means employed for its success, rather it entirely depends on its moral nature. Violence and non-violence are only the means to the success of that fight. Although the form of the action changes with deed or at the request of the doer, the request for some means does not change the moral nature of the request; because if one fanatical person takes the path of non-violence to prove himself, then his obsession cannot be called satyagraha or if a person fighting for truth commits violence for its accomplishment, then his fight for truth cannot be called fanaticism. If it was so, then what should the path of violence that Shri Krishna forced Arjuna in the Gita to accept for the accomplishment of truth be called?

- As a matter of fact, untouchability is such a terrible evil that there is no harm even if some people have to sacrifice their lives for its prevention. Just living is not everything. There are many ways to live. Even crows eat dirt and live for many years, but no one will say that there is value in their life. Why cry or panic about death? Sacrificing a mortal body in order to achieve something more eternal than this, for example, for the sake of the country, for the truth, for the goal, for fame—many great men have sacrificed their lives in the line of duty in many incidents. In the Mahabharata, Veer Mata Vidula preached to her son that it is better to show a spark of bravery for a few moments and die than to rot or live a hundred wasted lives. A time has come for every mother to give such advice to her son.
- I believe that it is in the interest of the nation to give rest to every mother for a specified period of time during the pre-delivery and post-delivery period.

- The principle of language-wise province composition is so vast that it is difficult to implement it practically. In case of accepting rationalism of this principle to its end, so many new provinces will have to be created that their number will prove the impracticality of that matter.
- One language, one way of life and one religion are the bases of nationality.
- If language-wise provinces have to be created, then the formula of one language and many states should be accepted and not of one state, one language. Due to the formula of one state, one language, the process of integration of North India and division of South India will begin.
- I have more love for Hindi, but Hindi-speaking people are the biggest and avowed enemies of Hindi and this is a matter of concern for me.
- Muslims are also minorities in Greece, Yugoslavia, Romania, Bulgaria, etc. But there are no separate constituencies. In Europe,

people of different religions and sects live peacefully as neighbours under the same rule without opposing a combined electorate.

- Even though I am a supporter of the idea that some sections should get separate representation, I am completely against the idea that there should be an independent electorate for this representation. The Regional Voters' Union and the Separate Voters' Union are two opposite poles. These two things should be completely avoided in the voting schemes which will be used to sow the seeds of a democracy-dominated state system in this country which lacks democracy. The solution to both is the combined electoral college system with reserved seats.

❑